ARS POETICA

Poems 2006-2013

Ivan Argüelles

◆

And vnderneathe the same a riuer flowes,
That is both swift and dangerous deepe withall

Poetry Hotel Press

Printed in the United States of America
Cover design by Clara Hsu
Cover painting: José Argüelles

ISBN 978-0-9891578-2-7

Library of Congress Control Number:
2013906329

Poetry Hotel Press
P.O. Box 347063, San Francisco, CA 94134-7063
www.poetryhotelpress.com

For James Balfour, my compatriot in the Blues,
who has shared with me the Mysteries of so many summers gone.

Acknowledgements

Some of these poems have appeared in the online magazines, *Caliban, Ginosko and The Tower Journal;* the title poem appeared in the anthology, *Poem, home* (2009).

CONTENTS

Introduction
by Jack Foley

"she is walking the other world?"
from *Ars Poetica*

Ars Poetica **is not a sonnet sequence—despite the resemblances—but a sequence of "soundings." Each poem is carefully dated: it was precisely at *this* moment that these words occurred to me; it was at this moment that I *breathed these words in* ("inspiration"). Remembering Wordsworth, we might call these poems *spots of time.***

Ivan Argüelles has produced a body of work rooted in his Mexican-American heritage, but it is unlike anything anyone in any ethnic group has produced. Initially grounded in the Spanish variety of Surrealism, his poetry swiftly began to transform itself into an instrument that communicates before it is fully—or sometimes even partially—understood. It is simultaneously "difficult"—restless, full of "references"—but also immediate, visceral. *It cannot be "explicated."* Moving beyond Catholic Mexico/Catholic Spain into the even darker roots of Catholicism, Argüelles' imagination explores the deeply pagan, deeply anarchic ground of an "other" tradition. Urban, sophisticated, learned in many languages ("tongues"), the poet creates a profane, stunningly transcendent, enormously erotic body of work that would probably have had him burned at the stake in the Middle Ages. Poet John M. Bennett insists that Argüelles' work "is not really 'literature' as the term is commonly understood": we must read it "with a new mind-set"; "one has to allow oneself to be 'drowned' in the ocean of this stunning and protean work and be receptive to all the ambiguities and contradictions it contains." Argüelles' own word for his work is "Enigma"; another way to describe it is to insist that it is a mystical consciousness which has removed itself from any known religion: San Juan de la Nada, poetry as *that old black magic.* Our critical categories fall by the wayside as we attempt to tell people what it is about this work that so moves us, that so "charms" us with its impossible, totally "inconsiderate" power and darkness:

"my" inspiration, year 1624
where is verdant luster, where
is emerald bay, not carbonized,
distance is the symbol, smoking
"that" famous cigarette, where
sidewalk turns into heaven's gate,
a remark in passing, lowering
head in gesture of shy naiad,
are there waters so crystalline?
distance is the signal, remote
the utter language of the Soul,
do the two recognize the Other?
++++++++++++++++++++++++++++++++
I don't remember what it is
("my inspiration")

We can call such passages "chaotic"—which they both are and are not. In its incredible swirl of sexuality, erudition, and massive longing, Argüelles' poetry asks the reader again and again, "You think you have an ego? Try *this*." But if we haven't an ego, what do we "have"? What the entity Argüelles calls his "Muse" has given him: an amazing language that simultaneously attracts and betrays us at every possible moment: "a music emerges a riot."

ARS POETICA

[... mountains, dreaming]

how it matters doesn't end
it where syntax glides obfuscated
crushed by a humiliating impact
the at first a poem situationist
green soft mauves a flash of pink
the gorgeous contralto voice
that dominates a Haendel opera
who hasn't wanted to just curl
up and die, every so often driving
around listening to "crazy for you"
out the window youth suddenly
altered by a whim called time
the one who dived into the
cement bath head first of course
whose sister was nominated Bach
candidate of the year but never
made it, small tokens memento
mori the whirring faces can never
remember their names who they are
which ones successfully wrote verse
which ones sick with envy, in a
suburb of mental anguish to the
right of the last telephone pole
behind the small stucco cottage
intent on the radio program
about Rapunzel, nicked several
times by the unerring blade the hero
whose imminence it occurs to me
a poem without a rhyme scheme

**or a suggestion that eventide
with its immense indefinable
melancholy watching trees fade
divested of color and ,
when we come back the next time
you with my face me with nothing
other than a memory you wore
once is it that you will not
relinquish it, not, when outside
others who pretended yourself to be
becoming terse as the planetary
metal shining dull against
the lifted water of a distance
that is called sleeping
++++++++++++++++++++++
either the opposition of night
or its epos in dark clusters
much like mountains, dreaming**

03-06-06

"this afternoon"

**how to express
the perfectly dumb anguish
sky overhead with its crown
of nothing, as of nothing
we are convinced will
ever happen beyond this
who has to say why
and who will die next
sorrowing on earth the round
and round bitter circle
repentant but of what
is the question, of course
a comes to mind doesn't it?
each has a syntax its own**

golden at times as dust
rushing out of the sun
at day's end or the time
you preferred not to leave
the theater, darkness as
numb as sleep in bitter
accents until lighted
for a last time the screen
with its pasted stars a
remote isn't it how disappearing
the land has no strength a
presence of nothing or
an absence of illusion
pointing towards a north,
why hadn't childhood a better
stay a purpose instead
of this chilling reflected
in a mirror of water
stagnant bronze-green
you can still hear the wings
whirring inches from the surface
but nothing does come back,
nothing is exactly in
the middle the still point
waking from a siesta
when each window becomes
precisely an unfamiliarity
difficult to pronounce
as if to see were a
but why go on, a situation
in marble dredged out of
the well of antiquity
for as soon as we are aware
it is also dark
the alone   how do
we?   for instance
an object or an angel
beyond human ken

3-5-06

[pre-socratic]

**an increase in grass
the size of air, where we
used to and gaze up at
sky in its infinite bedding
numbering by all accounts
what the Ionian philosophers
called a "perfect day"
each element in place and
color, from a side door
your future issued unawares
and unrecognized, brick by
brick the lesson graduated
into an invocation to the
"so called" Goddess who
in windows four flights up
appeared simultaneously
headless! which will be a
hue of choice, red, the
perhaps instant when you
dissolve, or I have not
remembered well the stage
upon which you walked in a
gorgeous soliloquy, the
passions it was called and
hand in hand the "other" assumed
too much, shadowless, swooning
into day's mercurial hour
glass of wine and a touch
of music, taking your hair
in its dreamy masses
darkness, at once, final
+++++++++++++++++++++++++
stepped off the mountain and
commenced falling, years
it took to reach the other side,
when looking for a definition
that would place distance
outside the Temple, was it
in your eyes? a golden suffix
to the verb "be" followed**

by the dusty steps impersonal
as is antiquity, beyond
++++++++++++++++++++++++++++
revolving around the supernal
"petit mal" trying to read
in the countenances who
escaped who nevertheless are
condemned to repeat, such
as sleeping on the higher
crests where bare scrub
trees lean against endless
the wind the fire the
far below not an echo,
how much eluded you in a
robe of stars and half-moons
the dance the initiation
breath and the infinite

(ii)

which fragment, from all accounts
sky a shadow lesser than before
a leap from flame to ether
and back to earth, dull clod
fragile in rain the
estuary drawing its current
from a "deity" into flesh,
the dreaming hill slope before
dawn who ushers forth sun's
unruly cart to draw like a
white plume across the azure
before plummeting, opaque
the glens where hide such as
have loved and fallen into
oblivion , patience
construed as an element "fuerza
del destino" , can metal
have such sheen can the heart's
arc be pulled so taut?
going out from the Door into
what dusty clime unshod who
seeks is it to question

the divide the tremendous
inert   , as clouds
are to sleep so man's mind
is adrift in a mirror dark
who cannot come back stepping
into the mortal stream
is it to be born the mystery?
+++++++++++++++++++++++++++++
music in the shattered ear
?
++++++++++++++++++++++++++++
to bring back bliss in hues
rose pink mauve the soft violet
the hawthorn white in its hedge
eglantine offered to the poet,
afar see the sea's crashing
waves the whiteheads the pounding
swooping the osprey and kingfisher
the raiment of gods aflutter
            high

03-21-06

[olympian]

as holy the entrance, utter disdain
roughing "it" with what stands for
distance a parking lot a high school
in flames the "girls" in their Lolita,
for once we misunderstand, for once
without comprehension at a sky
agape the crystal just breaks off
leaving us, trying to read the symbols
chinese for "leaving home" who bursts
out in laughter, clouds, the perhaps
a god in tinfoil looking for something
used, a sombrero, the bric-a-brac

of Apollo littered over the Sierra Madre,
unwholesome parts, who will reconsider
who will bed the self in lunar madness
who will at last, never mind, red is
the example given in the acting studio
her missive open to page blank, white
is the surfeit, in uneven columns
sort of lonely, as we all are, like
the time you shouldn't have opened
the envelope, love, often a sadness
a fog over the pane sets in, sleeping
is restless you wonder whose mate
has gone missing this time, automotive
and in a deep hiatus, greek with longing
an invitation to an intergalactic
ceremony, ennui, toothache, Minerva
with her stuffed owl, miles of dust
known as "White-armed Hera" before
the collapse the bright fluttering
awnings the rutting elephants drunk
in the motel courtyard chariots all
bestrewn along highway 101 south from
or almost beside the Acheron, flames
dusky as
evenings without you, promise to call
when you get "there",
            Temple harlots
withered garlands and weeping
cups of cyanide, a discarded notebook
with latin declensions in fine hand
a blueprint   morphine
languor
          immaterial whatever
you say about it, motes of light
named after stars, talking, talking
'til dawn the rosy fingered
++++++++++++++++++++++++++++
ex abrupto tossed off the cliff
was day ever so bright
              from afar
note their   tired
blurred vision, missed the stairs

threw a handful of
+++++++++++++++++++++++++++++++++++
is it to cry? is
conflagration
metal like “skin”
has to happen
only once
the otherwise corrupt
Text

03-09-06

[ends]

nor what ends, coming into the poem
into the exact meridian, white on
white dogwood and saffron side by
watering a night-wood, ends as
no sooner did she begin to speak AOI
sound of hooves trembling in foliage
of words indistinct, like gods who
have forgotten the way, whispering
each to the other about the One who
went before, the ending is somewhere
near the back door, near the small
well where the shadow weeping dissolved
to know, which is where, darkness
as a troubling of the spirit dusty
echoes of rust of, if you can Please
call me tomorrow, I think what
the doctor said is true, not that
angels in the clearing will signal
nor that
what’s the use, the Island, conscious
design carved out of the Blue
drifting   the incarnate
in gesso small and chipped paint

ending on the ledge, terracotta
a rough legend that is supposed to
mean   digging below skin
to find the song, to find something
of beauty or it is only a memory
like the day you arrived big at the gate
waiting for the ivy, for the hands
little as they were to open
up   section by
section near the wisteria, humming
a tune from the Last century
you went from bloom to bloom almost
radiant gathering what
for a while I believed then as days
turned into restless monotony
I began to forget, there is what
an ending is,   out of bounds
in a disguise powdery and evening
++++++++++++++++++++++++++++++++++
isn't it wistful the fade
turning to look a star in the corner
it is disappearing, end, ending pales
for whomsoever doth love fail

04-23-06

[fable of the bees]

longing is, a brief in green
leaves shooting in abounds of
sky the bluest immaculate
sphere we are in dwelling, of
grief the hemisphere left bleeding
somewhere over "there", other's
half on lawns imagined what
bright month, to the lamp
burning blame this self, hold as

owns to breast the trysting
"queen" in red, in notes crystal
as the hour's fixed night, or
a fiction drones implacable
on this waxen moon, whose chariot
the wheels work gyres before
plummeting into seas of,
what inky western heavens!
do no more ask of why these
verses rolling on so sudden
in their sting do halt, winged
sprite Oh my soul doth sorrow
tinge day's Eye and see what little
mourns the wounded bird, on high
sleeping in cloudy roar as if
ruddy waves to task a body's
infirmity and darkness yield,
++++++++++++++++++++++++++++++++
as if spinning, wet horizons
do wake? in the mind's buzzing
conscience labyrinths devour
such small light, grass, was
here lay beauty her fastened
song, skin, the rounds from
bloom to flowery weed and heath
the spore and honey dripped,
did we not here remain then
the morrow what would be?

05-04-06

[ars poetica]

angry that, Berenice's lock
doth no one show, who think
that to "get it off your chest"
is all, meaning of, sitting

**for hours for the noonday
class the wine growing tepid
the oblong shadow, of doubt,
of fear and the Man, over how
many days the epic struggles
first in hashed latin then
in obbligato cinquecento prose
finally as an after struck to
the unsounded chord, the rampant
shield aloft sun's glint the
Eye doth dart, hovering behind
clauses of rejection, pink stray
pages can go nowhere, isn't that
what? essentially at war with
syntax, with the elemental
emotion, ghosts, who rhyme
with darkness pleasure's ancient
ore, is it the peacocks in tumult
for rage and scorn alike?
is it for Mnemosyne the muse
of pearl-green hue?
is it for the variegated bloom
that adorns the suffix fair?
for whom is this catastrophe
of orange-red dust and powders?
is it heaven-sent we come to flail
among thunderstone and cliff?**

++++++++++++++++++++++++++++++++++

**who come to study not life
but its mundane chores and charnel
house the whores delectable a
prize in midden-heaps for those
that counting is the only game
for those who cannot above prose
rise, is it not hell their one
and only fane the boulevards
of littered prosody, come then
away to groves and shrines
where mystery, to dreams that
through cloud scrapes break!
here, admit "I do not understand"**

++++++++++++++++++++++++++++++++++

**is it to purple luster bruise
the Ear in sweet remorse doth tend?
how then does the assassin sing?
whence these Harpies to whom Meat
doth cling?   Ah No more
quod I in shrouded verse aspire
the elysian fields to espy
the dire moly and asphodel to eat
isn't that what warned us once
to remove from sight th'Infernal
and in meadows bleak to ply
the unsown shadows of dead the
angels who in Hell conspire**

++++++++++++++++++++++++++++++

**who will no more come summer's
plush to enjoy nor lake and mere
beside what slight waves in breeze
ruffled move in some small sleep
who dreaming in choirs vast
of languages radiant and beyond
gyres that tumbling round the
shafts of darker planet's score
warriors cleft from the Lamp
face down in miasmic gore, did
this one remember ever May's
bright? in hospitals gather
by bedside verse and to archaic
statues implore what Grief!**

++++++++++++++++++++++++++++

**is it to love the flower the many-
sided in winds swaying how sweet
remembrances in azure crystallize
and die
"remember Me" doth Narcissus
slake his breath in depthless Pool
doth Hyacinth then lament
upon his shepherd's rock
the day-long grass of tears
and rent his cloak in briars
running like one Mad
into the fierce Unknown
is it to love then, Heart?**

how words woven take on their own
subsiding never,
+++++++++++++++++++++++++++++++++++
now recline and die Thy little death
it is to Love, was once by might
taken suspended High above
while in the foaming spent of eons
the years unnumbered went
+++++++++++++++++++++++++++++++++++
"doth ever Rose so swoon and pale?"

05-10-06

[imitation]

shallow grave, stitches, this wood
anew doth strive, thy Heart forsake
thy bosom die, for why these reds
in cornices with mould grown o'er?

would it? shall never know the cross
mind's double fold, while sky's Lamp
into its grave doth speed, ken Ye not
such ample sleep no brain can contain?

whom didn't you forsake, nor crying by
what meadow's green did steep your tears
drowning such shadow profligate, why
wouldn't you deny? do then cloud the Eye

to realms stygian imply the Soul, for vast
and numberless the mystery, shades flitting
numb, shaking with Love's ague dumb th'inert
Maid disconsolate, twas Thee! in wax sealed

suggest to die, yellow, fie the Bright
one who stole from dream's Delight thy

purse, thy balm, thine Oriental flight,
do never more look back? slight song

slighter still the Anima in which wept
and grieving more, wakes? tongue's suchness
cannot pronounce, who weary wander out
beneath the tented Stars, Bells, Slippers

dew breaks crowns and steal away grasses
forever More! will't damn the Day? will't
in soft dialect the Body's jewel eschew?
how am I wrought from dross and enamel pure

how to traverse these Spaces ruddy? doth
lowly moan the aggravated, count then what
'pear to be the Comet's intellect, show
what cloth is the dappled song's only Skin!

for are we not as such? do we not but quake,
whenever I go back, there, ghostly firmament
the, aches, dolorous feint to trouble Thee,
once just more, then respond to marble Blank

evening sets more Pale, so White, so far
across each Longing, sighs, the archaic Stone,
the Bloom that echoes, why ever so? who
can at the door be if not Love's Mystery?

05-11-06

[love's echo]

what the word for it, is, passage
from the routine darkness into
lunar landscape, labyrinths, water
at once guessed then forgotten, who
dance round the symbol, forget,
do not come back, unless in the

memory of the Other, the opaque
shell out of which, hearing, a sea
on the beach reddens, twilit fires
in the mind's embryo, night, still
whispering into a net, hair cascades
down the shoulders whose pearly skin,
looks up to the mask, a planet
flares in dusky distance, cannot
hold, what is held out, falls once
the dream with its shaking branches
touches, against the glass breath
leaves its alphabet, if to reach
through this hour of sleep, if to
succumb to desire's inch of, why
did you not turn when the radiance
struck? lingers, trying to spell
exactly what, moving as if shadows
through rooms of gleaming merchandise
none of it ours, none who can,
in the next chamber, rushing sound
of reeds, a vacancy is announced
by an unseen god, small mouths
against the wind,
smaller still the aching because
+++++++++++++++++++++++++++++++++++
which is the one, which belongs to
no other, which is best removed,
why, months pass into waning years
yellow, then fade, a pale evening
when you find out, what,
knocking like silver, rust, I am
returning, I am
a ghost, myths adumbrate in the
underneath, steps no more heard,
silence
++++++++++++++++++++++++++++++++++++
(the) crystal

06-23-06

[ave atque vale]

**the last time, if ever, the lawn
either a sky or distance, itself,
who musing upon these matters, who
chasing into the dark, secrets better
kept, the unknown which sunders the,
flames eat the house, twilight or
its Other, buried beneath memory's
brief bric-a-brac, for example
when you answered the summons not
realizing how much Light was required
how much depth, frames of water glimpsed
rapidly, white, red awnings aflutter
in the square, a city of instances
a mirage, for hours the desert
extends backwards into a minaret
of shades, half the body was exposed
to night, the other half to a day
of fractions, no understanding why,
each one picked through the debris
certain of the answer, sirens in sleep
or in dishabille, removing piece
by piece the clothing, only skin
the impenetrable song, to be alive
+++++++++++++++++++++++++++++++++++++++
to be at wit's end, suggestions on a map
of the Stone, mysterious the voices
that live in the Ear, come with me,
please, come with me, dying because,
++
for a while you keep watching, a crowd,
consumed the moon like a fog-ridden
fiction tilts enlarged in the glass, then
a sea of remote lyrics, untranslatable,
no wonder the hand seeks to end, amaze
at clouds slowly shifting, to form**

07-09-06

[end of the world]

takes less time, three days? a
few words of lucidity, before
darkness the fell sets in, eyes
that never saw, nor does light
in its vast meandering receive
the mind's swift question, a sense
that all is at an end, that is what,
is ending, minute by minute, collapsed
in dust, storms of tiny fires dot
the celestial rim, who is talking
at once is not, the able come and
go making sense, others puzzled
eat the fray by the window, shades
ancient as grass lay down, evening,
hours pass, the shape of things,
even more distant the columns
irregular that mark years, yellow
followed by rust, red flush at
the corners of a city, to be, sad
conscripts of memory lined up like
verbs, can a hand hold such, does
the remnant of tongue recognize
the Syllable, unfolds in cascades
of water invisible what went on,
against bent rushes the wind,
sleeping, or not awake again, never
for a moment the indisputable issue
of breath, corrupted by the thin white
strip, heat that swells the members,
echoes of planets rounding out
a final fade, disorientation
++
rubble of words, as if dredged from
unfathomable depths, as if definitions
were exhausted limestone quarries, self
as a torn wing, into the flame
++
is it saturday afternoon?

night careless of memory's tomb
rolls on with its immense cloud
into the other world, into
the unknown
(for esther fulsaas, RIP)

07-26-06

[rg veda]

in her summer ghost a Hindustani girl
came up to me, snake charmer, wisp
of a thing with nothing on, a fold
or two in time, later in a deep haze
drifting inches above old Benares
my mind emptied of all things, red
and its illusion, white and its pacific
blank, blue deepening in the shape
of a god, her transversal flute like
a fire in my single ear, who am I
to ask? is there a first time for love?
a chance to smoke something illegal,
Bang! together we went shopping
in the ruins of Mohenjo Daro, she
wanted that crimson cloth a thousand
years in age, myself I desired
nothing, and nothing desired Me,
for hours in the same filthy hole
naked and sweating we poured out
the dregs of our souls, skin came
to shine, Song! derelict animals drunk
on our slime began to sleep, holy the
end of time, holy the unremembered Sound,
holy the instance of infatuation
++
dreams, ancient as the footprint, dust,
we are come to Kapilavastu, we are become

as archaic rock with engravings, who
can remember to turn off the light,
who will wake the inn-keeper?
+++
by late afternoon when the muezzin lies
dead in his wife, when the ox-carts come
to a puzzling stop, when nothing stirs
but the remote leaf buried in stucco, when
+++
one is for dying, one is for the thing
in the middle, one is for nothing, so
she said
two is for the grace of breath, two is
for the thing in the middle, two is for
nothing at all,
three is for Light
so she said
dropping one by one petals of snow
until from a distance that comes
without speaking, darkness

08-24-06

[john donne]

white side under goes
bleached blank the frame
music in its 17th century
resounds its unsounded Note
to name such things to sleep
in the beneath whorled leaf
sundered from the starry throng
mind's single core relents
wake then Thou! worm devour
heart's restless entity alive
in search of what underbrush
turn each blade around its green

**link to nerve its everyness
the holiday of aching dolorous
will we pine then in the hostel
wearing each other's wretched
skin a mask of flame and dross
the smoking cadaver in your eye
will it not wait for the avenue
with what tense invoke the Holy
being and its unexplained event
such is hush the eventide
its instrument yet now dulled
why the glass in its bleeding
light why the merry-go-round
its painted tigers whirling
in the eccentric lamp of time
do sit then Soul and nod off
reckon as no more the day
when thought creates its Air
move then around Love's pyre
and sitting for the hour whole
divine which is the entrance
and which the exit of Paradise**

09-15-06

"life is the same as death"

***news from portland is hospice care
and from coleman florida ditto***

**why did I ever give up smoking?
am I not the same as not being I
which is the puzzle and which the fix
accordingly descend with the Poets
to that gyre where the Prophet sizzles
holding his entrails in one hand
and giving benedictions with the other**

**can it be otherwise each morning
waiting for the messenger
when there is nothing to repeat
nothing to interpret
looking for the other bank of the River
hidden in some lyric fog**

**mistaken for a loud radio boulevard
cruising with Girlfriend from hell
whose tattoos are a cosmic design
ineffable ink passion intaglios
stricken with stage fright by the Song
how am I to proceed untied
blank presage in mists and
who can ever say I stepped here
nor whether it was my shadow talking
to the "other" night after night**

**all encompassing starlight falling
short of the inch where a name
dissolves before it can be memorized
alternate wave lengths reaching
out from the fifth dimension**

**a public library in the basement
where a plan of the accident
driven a mechanical device
right through the bone
a wonder he could walk again
to ask of the dead what is**

**stepping gingerly on the vast meadow
when aurora has slaked her horses
with waters of the Lethe
dew turns crimson that no eyes
turn to see if that is Hector
or Achilles braying at the Hour
but if you hold tightly to the reins
on the left side of the skin
a small mark an incision**

writing the poem was the poem

the intent was to go beyond
not what literature has to say
but what it cannot say
who are the derivatives
rattling spears of ash and dung
in the dingy suburbs of Limbo

I am the avenue and the way
neither to this side nor that
everybody is a window
nobody can see past the reflection
where darkest sublime feeds
on the roots of fire
where in the event of an accident
or an inflammation of the brain
the universe proves the Random

sitting in the same room forty years
are not developed
have not sung
is not being nor are others
insidious pornography of art
rearranging the non-existent

can you hear me?

09-13-07

(redhead at AMOEBA)

I am at the beginning of time
Onged with Buzz of early Beethoven
punk saws through leather souls
awl and stitch brain's seething
a component of Love detached
crawls down the sawdust aisle
into early Stonehenge crime ward

with litter of music fist in air
the Crimean War startles its berlioz
out of coma in 21st century when
who at the end of the whole of time
but the redhead who runs cash register
“hello!” like a Bang Bomb in skull
crushes the folded paper of lust
instilled like a dull blade in
the vein or else it is bourgeoisie
patched together like boiled denim
on top of the afternoon fix heat
sweat pops the brow in holocaust
of a dozen dead girl-bands whose
loud cacophony creates Boulevards
of illusory hollywood pornography
“willt have my heart, Dear One?”
the Duke of Earl falls brain-dead
below the revolving crimson matrix
is it how we resolve Venezuela Oil?
is it the distance to Teheran Hotel?
who is the avatar in the window fade
the longing cousin of orient sex
that brings Her? She? sewn to her
skin a casual song a tattoo refrain
the undergoing to hell and back
traffic of midstream noon wine
who never return to “tell”
who in fell Circe’s embrace do dream
twas ever thus in old Babylon
unreal hair redder than antiquity
++++++++++++++++++++++++++++++++++++
for how many seconds transfixed
to a glass of cold fate I spelled
this intricacy of glances and lies
twins between two frozen moons
circling her unutterable membrane
turns her back to show spine of china
massive dead wall of foreign devil
marching in trance through hong kong
bone-text tissue paper steam drill
++++++++++++++++++++++++++++++++++++
thus am I lost in music’s sublime

lighting at each end of the dark
resemblances to an afternoon identity
each is who, not one or the other
love's radiance
love's enormous
echo

09-21-06

(virgil)

is it that, a little wonder how
these so many years, without light
the origins have disappeared in a
heat and dust beyond sleep's hapless
definition, you was that Angel
suspended above a mirror of darkness
suspended above the hitches of hope,
I dared not survive buried in
the hexameters of antiquity, bark
of dead mariners in motionless mist
moving toward what emotion, north
of the body's axis, burning burning
in the pitch of music, cannot recall
the sound, Lilith? inches past the
first hour the one of dread where
grassy night empties in salt dreams,
Ear fixes its remnant Mnemosyne
whose ivy attaches to shadow going
listless and numb into the wall
+++++++++++++++++++++++++++++++++++++
parataxis of the void, in silk clouds
linger the seraphim in anguish gilt
to rain upon the rolling waters of,
thunders low the saturnian herd
hard by the shepherd's Tomb, arise
then the nymphs in drugged torpor

**for whom the promised boulevard's
shiny radio is meant, then to tuscan
tufa mounds the hills begin their
august sweep, each morning is less
a hint of the end drawing smoke,
by evening sundered halves aching
ask for their souls back, return
no more under earth the grinding
worm, slopes sparsely marked by
oxen drowsy white 'neath arcadian
foliage noon-drunk, wine pressed**
+++++++++++++++++++++++++++++++++
**is for the distant bell, a sign
moving through the mind's labyrinth
until in the forum's mid morning
in haggard dialect the Stoic ceases
his argument, "you may remember
but Once this day, come back no more"**
+++++++++++++++++++++++++++++++++++++
**quivering in the damp conifers
a goddess naked for no reason known
removes the minute song from her
rent hair, combs ivory-toothed
and brooches carved from bone litter
the place she has stepped, alpha
the forlorn**
++++++++++++++++++++++++++++++++++++
**to the storm at sea, to the husky winds
hollowing out night's craven desire,
to the blank and dense cliff
let sound the small rain
beneath which these pages burn**

10-05-06

(alba)

**what was that, mad, I thee implore
past the heaven-gate, beyond afric's
wildest sand, I am a temple Dumb!
for thee askance these waters skirt
the endless realm, a mantra nightly
exports dim night's final hour and
Lo dawn's hush a vague tumult below
the Ear, insane islands
silence of each, transformed Thou
into a tiny shell dost slide flow
forth into sky's smallest chamber
there wait, hunh? shores
of antiquity , elegant you was
in spotless raiment strutting up
there on cloud number Nine, I took
you for an angel, a music of intense
as many sounds it takes to fill a
year, the entire spectrum from red
to ultraviolet, Big Bang, shuddering
infinity waves, a finger
implores to have you back, Thou,
a palace of second guesses windows
the subaltern I have become a regret
that life does not, however little
its rain spots the immense metal,
waking, at least not sleeping more
begin to look past the escarpment
where noon readies its whitest arms
++++++++++++++++++++++++++++++++++++
intercept the Achaeans as they round
the bend, day's third watch brightens
each distant tower, a promise war will
today end, this brief skirmish, ages
++++++++++++++++++++++++++++++++++++++
wearing see-through skin and blanch
as clusters of eglantine her face a
roseate pale blank, is a wonder to
confirm the odyssey hers is a walking
into darkness unbeknownst, take my
hand , promontories of gas**

the legend of the Egyptian Helen
+++++++++++++++++++++++++++++++++++++
histories erased by, lipstick, garters
and high-heeled shoes, goes by weaving
light and for just an instant am I
in rapture, was Thee ever so lorn?

10-12-06

(theseus)

the not quiet, who are burning
beside the Self, alone, or with grief
wandering the sunless slopes as if,
who waking know not where and next
to the Monday without end, who
will keep burning outside the Self
the witless, though I am with “them”
though I am in tears submerged, who
when eventide shrouds day’s eye
and no more returns the Shepherd,
it was then the smoke to heaven sent
and from afar the Ships! one day
with them shalt Thou tarry, such a
summons in small voice through
the rent wall heard I, hurrying
as if to open for once the Door
as if, but who beyond the Self walk
lost in groves of asphodel and lime
slaked by asbestos quickened to end,
who amongst the throngs of listless
cigarette in hand with ear alert, am
this I, questions sleeping the unuttered
mouth, the soundless vowels, clouds
++
it is not to speak, nor to the deaf
lend voice, Stranger, but in bottomless

where wave and wind mingle darkly
there respond to light its wing,
shake from dreams the Unspoken, who
in hospitals with bell jar and ringing
search hopelessly, who once green and
singing of skin the Loud, ah 'twas for
them I went forth nameless, with whom
the dead share this music   the high
absolutely,   boughs wet
++
spinning, the gauze invisible breaks
even the Sunne's great ray, shivering
sends into glassy water the distant
who are not slaked, am I coming home?
thus   a red thread tying to the Port
this reminiscence   this absence

10-14-06

"about what is poetry"

after all these years
to pick up a book and
remember what it was like
"les neiges d'antan"
fewer regards for "that"
a bride selected for her
antidote to philosophy
of darkness and the Man
I sling each into its void
the nevertheless nothing
raging and you ask
"what is it you carry?"
"in this bag are 2 thousand
years of war and madness"
thus we have not far come
is a river we imagine

spooling mid willow and
groves shady darkening
past noon a full minute
bedded in grass and thyme
in whose lap are recalled
assonance of gold and
above stars heavy with
a nomenclature of beauty
and despond, skin
+++++++++++++++++++++++++
is it not easier to forget?
you were the one posing
as the Quean of Hell far
from right in nothing but,
each section labeled for
a disease or hopelessness,
in which abyss bleeding
for what unknown "thing"
as years go by whispers
like moths eat your eyes,
such as winds of what
aching regrets of song
oriental flooding the ear,
is a sea beside itself
preying on glass entities?
+++++++++++++++++++++++++++
in which quadrant of the sky
will You be when it's done?
what will be your
Signal?
+++++++++++++++++++++++++++
precious the few who love

10-28-07

(“nikki” elegy)

**how false was the, skin?
across the stage voice like
a diamond, cutting through fog,
a distance, followed by still
another distance, lights dimmed
for the ovation, flowers, years
in growing, by the time this
reaches You, a dream in which
through a glass, younger than
recalled your hands, far from
being, your mouth fresher than,
inches of grass, the pavilion
bathed in a crystalline, moon,
stars alphabetically arranged,
offered you a book, the Book,
ancient verses illegible in
their faint cuneiform, chinese
ink dried on the margin, red,
who will die of ovarian cancer,
despite Love, the kabuki actors
each with a role to play about
You, versifying the loci where,
interpretations are a pallid,
+++++++++++++++++++++++++++++++++
mountain, rills of pure, rock
and quartz, sandstone, pine,
dew, black the wet boughs weigh
against evening, dying, a mask,
the Pleiades swooning, have lost
formation, not far from the ocean,
an origination of things, whisper
++++++++++++++++++++++++++++++++++
Call me, if you’re able**

11-05-06

(redhead at AMOEBA ii)

**is it each who has the other?
has no other, than the obsessed,
voice of a woman, wisely dressed
as a doll in red hair, who turns
to the emblem in the air, speaking
as if no other, her flashes at me,
I die in the course, puzzled that
will limit my understanding, voodoo
in see through skin, reductio ad
absurdum, they say, seized and
truncated by a whim, music vast
as the ether, surrounded by wall
of watery silence, heat, the great
fish of the Father peering, glass
no longer holds, red is enormous,
more than the other, I who am that,
across some vedic norm, shall we?**
++++++++++++++++++++++++++++++++++
**dancing, not dancing, fiery shores
"do not approach", her, between
the lies of breath, behind light's
semblance, her, other is renewed,
denied, other is her, switches
money in the form of desire, void,**
++++++++++++++++++++++++++++++++++++
**forbidden fruit, crimson, delicate
skin, the song, what is the face
behind the, shades, ashes, her is
what is beyond the other, approaches
to what is, being now, crimson, or
vermilion in the hair, parted for
a way of non-being, or twined in a
long braid, unobtainable, like the
great wall of china, falling, her,
as is the other, in whose eyes a
myriad, not the other, gleam, not
a promise, nothing, her, "follow
me" echoes spoken to so many, others**
++++++++++++++++++++++++++++++++++++++
unapproachable, a demon, whose voice

has she plundered, whose eyes, whose
skin whose whose whose, madness at
the forefront, please buy this music
++
it will be, other, her, under the
chiffon blouse, a

11-08-06

(redhead at AMOEBA [in black])

startled by the at once, cognition
like fireflies in a sudden, darkness,
all around wall of "sound", deaf
to the otherness approaching, as
if by a magnet drawn to the lack,
zero, void, cancel all regret,
hanging in the air, or not being
at all, a rush of blood to the
surface where the signature waits,
a thing, amalgam of memory and
untruth, immense as the red of
sleep, as the red behind the mirror,
it is to puzzle, is it that hands
are intelligent, that a part of
history is smooth, women seated
like jewels in the corners, both
infantile and mature who watch or
who do not, unexpectedly dressed
in black, taller for the distance
between language, music disguised
as hair, painted in order to be
exotic, faint dead away in the
chrysalis, hoodoo, floods rising
in the kingdom, waters aching
to know, You
++++++++++++++++++++++++++++++++++

**nameless, the entity in the worm,
halves of moon dislocated almost
loud, wandering in the store like
Handel in Israel, angel stops to
fix his hips, straighten his wig,
replace his tooth, dies, a manner
of speaking, angel is paper flame,
a longing inside the credit card,
what cannot be returned, note by
solemn note, under the text, read
it backwards, say "thank you"**
++++++++++++++++++++++++++++++++++++
**opened, slowly, each syllable a
part of the other, next time is
a question**

11-14-06

(proserpina at AMOEBA)

**cannot unfold, deeper sections cut
though crowds in silence mourn, white
on white, up and down the stairs,
legs like water, all the things that
can go wrong, who she is, the fast
identity inside the music, chorals
of angelic resound, waiting, as if
to signal "going down", ringing
in the Ear, smiles in shifts like
colors in empty light, how is it that
hair, eyes with heavy shade of blue,
reddens the invisible, "your boat is
small / cannot hold up to the Great
Seas", down among the disembodied
voices, further down going fast,
entelechy of love? the smart thing**

to do is go back, up the stairs,
into the air, smothering ether
where the stars each, unremembering
the name, stand by me, beside the
column of rushing water, whispering
to the Soul, harp, viol, lyre
++++++++++++++++++++++++++++++++++++
have taken from the body this weight,
released breath, now rocking dry
of mouth, pale she, what is once
recalled, forget everything else,
she who like a feather in amber,
deriding the gods in their distance,
who is unnumbered, her, knocking
against what can never be seen,
sounds, will I ever be so bold?
++++++++++++++++++++++++++++++++++++
drum-head, tattoo, nose-ring, jade,
in small doses, how many words in
Italian does she know? bacchant
ululating in monteverdi's Orfeo,
maddening, as the crimson she wears
for a mind, behind each wall, ghostly
+++++++++++++++++++++++++++++++++++++
to Hades, whichever way one looks,
disregard, beauty, to memorize
her skin, the song, to count how
far it goes, echo's longing

11-19-06

(euridice [redhead at AMOEBA v])

called out, looked back, second
guessed, all color drained from

but for the hair, crazy red,
an instant blind to the “thing”,
memory went short, halt, fewer
littered the bed of thoughts,
infatuation with the dead or
with impossibilities breathing,
as it is, no longer informed
of body or text, simply moving
between spaces, seven invisible
heavens, antiquity, where all
are shades, formless of mind,
to name them the “spirits”, who
assume endlessly the Body, who
as a corpse falls to earth, who
shift in the scheme of color
the implausible Light, above
whose head a lamp shines like
the evening of regret, like the
+++++++++++++++++++++++++++++++
absent though walking, still,
sidewalks lit by cigarettes
and the traffic din of Noon,
white, whiter yet the wine
chilled to the death, each music
lifts the nameless, clouds of
incense unfurl violently as if
calling to the abyss, asbestos,
asphodel, planets that govern
the Hour in its dread, disappear
++++++++++++++++++++++++++++++++
sheets unwound where faint print
remembrance lingers, yellow stain
the blouse she wore, what remains,
unseen, in the cuneiform of air,
passing through darkness into
darkness, away from the world
and all that “seems”,
+++++++++++++++++++++++++++++++++
isn’t it time to come home?
lost in the fury of painted albums
in the resentment of aisles

in deep bins of unrecorded sound
does nothing return?

11-20-06

(MUSE)
for the redhead at AMOEBA

what god isn't invisible?
what plague, what source?
doth heaven reign? afternoons
in hell with a Favorite,
the muse in her interlocking
panoply of hair, red, enormous
as dreams, or as the descent
from the last of the heavens,
do we believe in reincarnation?
after how many buddhas is
perfection? a lake lifted by
levers to Pure Land, swift,
the instantaneous glance,
discomfort and its inflection
by way of bel canto, flames
higher than the moon, Beauty,
what is this pallor, this?
by what intention does it
become mid-afternoon and why?
look, from afar banks of flowers,
where does it come from?
unpronounceable, the hermetic,
oblivion, these things gliding
towards us, unobtainable as
are mirages, their colors
saffron unique turquoise azure
fade, phantom on the water,
++++++++++++++++++++++++++++++++
if it has a name, call it forth,

history is a circular ruin,
rust and what lies behind it,
is it we are dizzy recounting
these previous births, what matter
the myth of the Swan? going into
the unknown the dark spectral
what matter, does Muse askance
see through the glass “other”
things? rushing avenue in smoke
all beings become imperceptible,
forty arhats in each direction
a riddle, rite of fire and
+++++++++++++++++++++++++++++++
muse is candy floss is diamond
is much the different muse than
music allows for the powerful
suggestion of muse in tight and
watching darkness reveal its once
distinction of alpha and omega
muse is, temple roof collapse
rain and fog obliterate horizon
Sublime isn’t it?
has everything been said?
+++++++++++++++++++++++++++++++
“love’s illusions everywhere”

11-21-06

(exalted)

perhaps, or fever pitch, unable
to breathe as before, the dense
rush of the hour is gone before
you know it, sand eddies darkness
in wine, physical evidence gone,
the merely empty artifact confused
with a one way memory, like the

time dressed in blue, looking for
red stripes, done up the hair like
a gondola, for however many instances
the photograph takes, music to be,
counts to zero in rapid french,
doesn't linger long before inches
take their toll, heaving aside
matters of history, smoother and
less obvious, rooms open up lateral
with stars painted at either end,
night at two in the afternoon!
investigating vermillion, columns
of dizzying light, fortune to
see You, and grace, smallest rain
++++++++++++++++++++++++++++++++++
one is for skin, two for the indigo
match, three suspended in space,
forever falling from dream into
dream, whom angels narrowly miss,
painting the color of substance
the masses of fiery air, in a minute
all is reduced to ice, single
and devouring, sleep in the angle
best suited for standing "alone"
+++++++++++++++++++++++++++++++++++++
five is for the number a body never
knows, the heat between two lives,
the engine within the music, six
is at last Never, the rest are beyond
the pale, a migraine, a sorting
booth, a situation without clouds,
why is nothing, where is the resolve,
does oil catch fire easier than air?
+++++++++++++++++++++++++++++++++++++
when dark chooses to remain, when
within the inch whole lives transpire,
when each time I come back, what
is a peninsula of gas, what is the
story about this time, repeatable
incisions, passion, dolorous acts
caught on tape, why is no definition
+++++++++++++++++++++++++++++++++++++
OK you got it, circling ever faster

**above planet Gaia, no feet to walk,
no hands to hold, temperature beyond
the meridian, each ambulance a jet
of seraphic flame, it has no exit,
only the luminous transcendence that
flashes each time You come into view**

11-23-06

_(F*A*D*E)_

**not deliverance, not the other shore
the fading, one at a time loss, one
more day small rains, washing color
out of daylight, nor redemption, nor
the fires in the heart, fading, smokes
the chill, glass becomes opaque not
reflecting, other rooms governed by
cold statues, other vistas beyond
the horizon, fading, ultimate things
unnumbered, unremembered, what story
was being told, over "there" red reborn,
out of ashes flung over the bay, echoes,
out of the uninhabited, from each depth
fading, like aspirin, moon's plangent
halo adrift, exiled stardust, a poem
recited, some chinese annotations about,
fading relentlessly, about the drizzle
this afternoon, about what is left
after the storm, each leaf torn from
a voice, without identity, chalk dust**
++
**no recall, walking the grassy nowhere,
listen, the fade, a blank cartouche,
the dream, similarities between void
and blanch, someone staring from afar,**

ridge and hummock, tufts of osier and
reed, each foot sinking in the mire,
whose fading mask a memory bore to
no one, hand little matters, air gravely
dun colored, fading, shapes lose form,
angel crashes, somewhere outside the Hour,
behind the clump of charred, hush,
hear that? cloud bank moving out above
++++++++++++++++++++++++++++++++++++++
stillness, no nearer than sleep, out
ever shifting, fades, lingering a soft
ending to thought, a never, a shade,
as the names of rivers, fade, as evening
turns into dust, white darkens white,
shutters collapse on empty glass, fading
masks, echoing prints in a loss, powders
crimson filtered through a dream, who
++++++++++++++++++++++++++++++++++++++
is it ever over with? do the "others'
understand? beside fading green a pure
blank issues: moon, planets of antiquity,
the "archaic" animal, asleep, a fade, a

11-27-06

(sublime, the)

coming up again, towards light
unwithering, whole spheres
on fire above, weightless
like the soul,   have we been
so fortunate, asks the "other",
no regrets   whitening
shines, what is early and red

flush at odd angles, angel
in proportion to   blank,
descending darkness
++++++++++++++++++++++++++++++
vow to keep to the shore, waves
torment   republic of day
adrift in “that”, fog, careens
hiding the   who suddenly
manifest reborn bright, distant
however the smile, archaic
and walking to   , sunset
in aisles of pepper grove and
tamarind   dusty echo,
who have not yet from sleep
come forth,   in mountains high
the icy breath, asunder for a
moment the soul’s halves, sigh
in the Ear great longing   ,
+++++++++++++++++++++++++++++++
a song, followed by skin   dim
the eerie, twilight in the rushes,
lapping of water, whorls cinder
colored eyes   , what is waiting
spear in hand   am I to
for once understand?   edges
around which the planet circles,
rust   silver, ague thinking
what is Love to be,   rock
formations   fern-print, a
fever   or breath aflame,
near the house a path, who reach
into the night   who wearing
crowns of invisible   ,
++++++++++++++++++++++++++++++++++
music of cymbals and small bells,
on the soles of their feet tattoos
vermillion   , or wear the
hair in   vertigo, like
the ships bearing the dead

**to this point are we come,
listen**

11-30-06

(tuesdays at AMOEBA)

**don’t tear the house down, burn it,
clouds, the ancient oracle turns
up the volume looking back, red
intransigence, layers of distance
unrepeatable and white, who will
answer to this traffic of dense
music, here, instead of a hand
the mind’s intense stare, yellow
washes out to sea, misty, azure
the hollow sky, more clouds lower
than allowed, sensory projection
in the Eye, copulating, frieze
of longing and harmony, unremembered
shores running the length of time,
is it that You have entered this
the twenty-eighth Mansion? light
in fossil increments, no hope,
but the mountain rears feathery
its peak on some orient screen,
all around fogs wrap darkening
twilight in the inevitable**
++++++++++++++++++++++++++++++++
**in no place known unravel sands
the eternal, suffice an accident
to happen, angel between lives
descending, horizons of mirage
and incapacity, who are making
their way to some inner Asia,
who keep to the dharma asking
no single One, speaking low in**

tones forbidden, askance the glance
that wounds, turn Away! does legend
forsake her cosmetics crimson
and powders, undressing dressing
in a reversed minute, skin flowers
like a myth in snow, does anything
happen behind the Door?
++++++++++++++++++++++++++++++++
vermillion is for antiquity,
the part in the hair, the holy,
whisper in the water what is
distant, what is lingering along
the way, what is longing, what is
++++++++++++++++++++++++++++++++++
mystery, lunar, what eclipsed
brain can "see"?   what
emotion, the unspeakable

12-03-06

(reincarnation at AMOEBA)

not as you think, entrance to hell
SE corner of Haste and Telegraph,
inches away born from the Lotus
redhead again in her intricacies
of twill and rust, is what follows
a version in yellow of a birth-tale
shape in darkness argent pullover
crimson where sight should be a
third of the time lost to night,
heavens rising seven-fold in mad
ascendancy over rush of sleeping
waters, dream flowers in an alphabet
located near Indus valley cemetery
dancing girls writhed in bone-text
until vermillion powders vast hair,

towers invisible and empty high
over the shaded lore the ineffable
+++++++++++++++++++++++++++++++++++
who are becoming large and wet across
the plains, moving archaic script
into the Eye, to read there a life
hagiographies small footnotes breath
everything tangled in green underbrush,
it is what light, it is a harmony,
what music sounds in inky reaches
distance and horizon collapsed
into a single rune of Night, shhh
+++++++++++++++++++++++++++++++++++++
when I will return when I will not,
demand neither money nor promise from
them, turn the face towards an orient
painted in colors of mist and fog,
each foot with its tattoo, each hand
as if to see the written volume, air,
in hindsight dying, a likeness, or
a scroll recording the leaves as
morning turns into its labyrinth
+++++++++++++++++++++++++++++++++++++
ivy fern dogwood hyacinth jasmine
who are there still, waiting, song
skin flame ether what abounds
the next life, and the next one,
++++++++++++++++++++++++++++++++++++
did I know you then? where were you
going in such white and rash of step
all sky around you fire and willing
done the thirty three illusions
folded the ninety nine paths of
alas! smoking mountain ash
buried the   ,
longing in flutes burning
spurn echo its return,
what grass doth then Eurydice
            pace?

12-04-06

(fragility of being)

**"take care of yourself," sure,
when traffic takes music to its
outer limit, falling off the sheer
like glass breaking in sleep, does
angel wrap around the automatic
weapon in order to see better?
is it because cold no longer fits
nylon, or the subject of red, once
the immense other version of the
universe, is reduced to a shop
clerk dressed in punk, is there
a need to "know"? who awake
stands on the verge exalted but
who can never say "why", answers
come in pills, midnight is exile,
lunch is a thing of the past,
hovers a wing ever so pale near
what extinguished light, be born,
exult! around the corner wearing
see-through skin Angel cigarettes
an audience of weary, head in scarves
indigo saffron ruby, whatever
comes closest to red, dying just
when the door, applause, think
twice before re-entry, windows
blackened for the infernal Hour,
tongs in hand the Master stairs
his intention, poetry, wild air
at the summit of a lost season,
mountains dreaming, mist, chinese
intaglios, delicacy of breath,
ice, shapes of ink, ivy darkens**
+++++++++++++++++++++++++++++++++++
evenings the soul alone, what small

remembrance life was, a hand lifts
the other hand, kiss, shadows that
longing fixes in a dream, yellow
or at once the impulse to versify,
no, it isn't what matters that's
important, hair, centrifugal flight,
oceans of space, maddened by some
whim in a scarlet kimono, until
only the whites of the eyes, dancing
or praying, nothing really, edges
fray, inches to go, BANG, short
by a year the Eye designates its
own distance, folds in a pattern,
love for example, or the sheets
hung out to dry, or nothing else
at all, but the sublime within
"the," willing to go undone, small
as rain on an unknown island
+++++++++++++++++++++++++++++++++
if the poem occurs, the inspired
tract circling in miasma, don't
go home, let the sun set of its
own accord, destroy the shopping
list, forget the other colors,
an aria from Julius Caesar, or
behind the screen a frond waving,
no egress but the sandy waste,
how long has it been since?
look away, sky,
+++++++++++++++++++++++++++++++++++
keep it mysterious,

for jack foley

12-07-06

(mnemosyne at AMOEBA)

once scattered on earth, light,
is it what matters entering
this Mansion, darkened music
altered for descent, looking
no other way for shadows in
defense, the suddenness of Red
positioned beyond the "other",
who in an act of levitation moves
one heaven into the next, ideal,
one remove from hell, five full
inches from Chaos, each brief
step into the opposite, mountains
of helium rear their olympian
ruin, below stars crash into a
redundancy of water swirling
madness, as it is to see You,
doth chaste Diana aim her bow?
doth Bernice her lock reclaim?
how doth then sweet Dido Burn!
such candies melt, such bitter's
smoking in disguise, how will
this island turn its realm
around and sinking, look high
the welkin's rolling purple
forge thunder loud revolves,
is it a verse to learn dying
on the ethereal stair? is far
from the cliff better drowning?
+++++++++++++++++++++++++++++++
small breath echoes arrow, lesser
still the white beyond, a pale
some form resides in flowering,
yet You, behind ramparts silent
in song's wild skin, return
hand in grass, foot in leaf, ivy
to its memory, eroding wall of
+++++++++++++++++++++++++++++++++
shock in tomb's sweet regret, wake
to steer the Eye into some soft
mass like Daphne's hair, crimson

with distance, whispered, gone
+++++++++++++++++++++++++++++++++
how many are sleep's feet undone,
myth, ineffable, dust, cloud

12-11-06

(Eleusinian Mystery)

more mysterious than ever, You,
in that fogbound vest of dream,
cloudy eye veers from cliff to
resounding cliff, or sounds sheer
that cut sleep from sleep, a vast
intricacy of dark, repeal voice,
cancel each petty syllable, each
whim in skirt and flower redressed
to frame the Hour, is it too steep
to go so fast? *which* is the whole
life just passed? murmurs echo
darkness near in years undone, how
more mysterious yet the You, who
transcendent in petals of light,
who in shades and flounces fading,
how is the name pronounced that
has never been heard? sweet, seems
sweeter yet the disappearing,
secrets, hush of violets asleep,
between what thin layers does
breath? running up country
++++++++++++++++++++++++++++++++++
does then a second left remain?
to whom address unwonted love?
how do so many fall from grace?
never having known, never being
seen, the unexpected, the
+++++++++++++++++++++++++++++++++++

kneel before the Invisible, listen
what stars kenning fate crash afar
in inky spaces gone, I am there where
not once was ever before, angel
dusting a trajectory undoes death
in a single inspired Note, then
itself dies again, unrepeatable,
unnumbered, uncounted, whiter yet
more mysterious for the pale, aside
++++++++++++++++++++++++++++++++++++
let the animal feed upon Thy hand,
whom no one doth Remember, whom
none recall how sleeping deeper still
She rent the cloth, cutting in half
fate’s thin black thread, doubling
by zero oblivion’s unseen mask
+++++++++++++++++++++++++++++++++++
do then step forth, hair a pomp,
red, darkening skin’s frail song,
“beautiful stranger”, all vanish
all from sight, into the vast,
into the unformed Beyond

12-13-06

mythology for the redhead at AMOEBA)

slim jewel cases, like waists,
gilt fringes argent clasps a
like heaven in similar clouds
whose heads appear the vague
a dreaming, slipped through
the lining torn, the ripped
seam out gushes rust in fogs,
one by one a goddess only
when foot on water steps ever
gliding like shadow, forever

**it seems the green cascade
in the Eye, have not seen like
this before a landscape rears
into a misty drowning, names
of the inevitable not uttered
nor for a deity masked as air,
how hovering masses of hair
moistened then disappear behind
mirror's lunar echo, arose
then from mere earth the serene
in her skin of shimmering, like
dew her voice in drops of harp
can one recall? green is here
a rush of ivy whispering alba
until at the glass, knocking
tips a wet branch to waken
what lies within the pearl's
dissolve, how paradise is
a summons to hear, but red
in swirling skirts of darkness
around the brace, why does it
not return? whose mystery sings
beginning over again, counting
from behind the enormous world
emerging shatters in its light**
++++++++++++++++++++++++++++++++
**each is a story, few in number,
then life has no answer, hers
is a page of aspirin or a head
constantly turned away, distress
on its horse before a grove
of secret, glass vibrates in
its planet of frost, noon comes
followed by the second Hour,
how little one cares to know
why evening is so sudden, gone,
who are sleeping nameless beside
the eminent shadow, when music
descends from its mountain white
appealing to the silent waves**
++++++++++++++++++++++++++++++++++
by midnight the full resonance,

intimate voices, what language
it is against pure stone and does
not, a poem, a myth in dust, a
fragrance of grass come into being,
another, if to speak were a
possibility, to create a shape
where only color becomes pure,
or is her face at the opposite
end of things what exists, alone

12-16-06

(“my” inspiration)

walking down the street, in hand
the famous cigarette, telegraph
anno domini 1624, slimmer than
at first remembered in skin the
size of song, does pain encounter
the rule of glass? does a chance
have seconds? why question what
regards looking askance, button
each flower to legend’s memory,
it is not here the mantra “works”,
not here the holiday becomes “modern”,
not here anything at all “happens”,
not here if not in december One
hundred years ago, frost inches
up the spine to numb any recall,
to think how suddenly Red acts
on the nervous system, light shuts
its window, darkness is an appeal
to frame the whole “thing”, is
it a secret to wear? is there
a somewhere behind the eclipse,
a paradise without function,
except for the stress on her

**accent, but for the day's eye
turning in her ineffable holy,
every sunday it is like a cosmos
imploding, four hours, then echoes
of silence in weird green waves,
inside a city fixes its Lamp,
waiting for ulysses to come home
nostalgic and great with shadow,
outside people gather waiting
for the municipal voice, a horse
potentially, a statue crying
for more marble, Eurydice,
in fact a music emerges a riot
of invisibility, inchoate sphere
+++++++++++++++++++++++++++++
I don't know why she is
I don't know why she is
I don't know why she is
++++++++++++++++++++++++++++
"my" inspiration, year 1624
where is verdant luster, where
is emerald bay, not carbonized,
distance is the symbol, smoking
"that" famous cigarette, where
sidewalk turns into heaven's gate,
a remark in passing, lowering
head in gesture of shy naiad,
are there waters so crystalline?
distance is the signal, remote
the utter language of the Soul,
do the two recognize the Other?
+++++++++++++++++++++++++++++++
I don't remember what it is
I don't remember who it is
I don't remember why it is
++++++++++++++++++++++++++++++++
"my" inspiration, are there better
words for it? can one "know"?
it is a mystery, for why is
everything so blank today,
for why is the sky, riches are
not wealth, beauty is for why,
mere cloud banks announce it,**

**thunder in the middle of the sun,
the edge is as near as it gets,
floral games, eglantine jasmine
hyacinth as prizes, swarm ever
the bees in their mock summer,
climbs the ivy in its dream
of dense verbiage, darker yet
the inch between annihilation
and the declaration of love,
darker still the river beneath
++++++++++++++++++++++++++++++
darkest breath instills
some white smallness
is it that no longer "here"
she is walking the other world?**

12-17-06

(AMOEBA house of mystery)
for michelle

**down darkest stairs, inferno's
turn left from right first stage
smoking, who is in front door-side
rust colored for bright effects
and hair done-up for wild, shifts
no ordinary light her eyes, look,
always a surprise to be alive,
again, animals rather than spirit
drinking in obscurity, it is to
be salvaged by tons of music
recycled and unexpurgated, *"my
boy friend's back,"* when really
nothing matters, each tone drives
china a year farther away from
its voice, shattered by the as
it were, beauty highlights skin**

**in opulent however faint turquoise
until song splits in two, one
is for the monkey in redress,
two is for the "habit", taking
rounds between antiquity and its
ruins, three is for the eternity
hinted in her emerald glance, a
brief deity whose purpose is green,
but whose tooth alarms dusky air
with the approach of loss, silver
++++++++++++++++++++++++++++++++++++
rather than walls, imagine, junk
detritus the wholesale infirmity,
ready to collapse, the unsure
melody about shores and twilight,
fog dense as a french overture,
wearing her red kimono before
diving head first into despond,
how is it angels manifest, cloudy
in a winter of aspirin colored,
back and forth with price wars
and the average age of planets,
that is sudden, a rush to the
heart, blood expensive as time,
blank, issues of forged currency
++++++++++++++++++++++++++++++++++
they are having at the slave,
pinned to the surface of paper
and after all these centuries
shining, account for nothing but
the falsetto, who are not there
who have not learned their lesson
who are forbidden, alphabet noise,
if you go upstairs it is the end,
but to return downstairs wear
absolutely nothing, oratorio
about seraphim inoculated against
Pleasure, venereal triptych
++++++++++++++++++++++++++++++++++
the painting suggests a woman
whose known orient is a disguise,
around skirts of ruddy opium,**

or an immense cigarette about
to go "off", salvation ditto,
footnotes with bodhisattvas
++++++++++++++++++++++++++++++++
impermanence non-self

12-19-06

(crazy : footnote)

crazy, every time I see you
I want to write a poem, maybe
one day we can go to hollywood,
together, and see how the store
there is, see how it "works"
in the absence of rhyme, just
a cigarette and home-sickness,
like in the old days, before
crime was the issue, the scarlet
letter worn in braids, loud,
music every inch of the way,
pushing mountains into view,
big purple haze, madness isn't
it? like every time I walk in
and you're standing there in
shrouded myth, a template of
gorgeous hair crowns your very
thought, from you the Idea
springs of the eternal sphere,
of the ether where spent planets
circle, dizzy, where the archaic
becomes the ever present, who
step after step die unto Time,
who do not regard what is around
them smoking the dense, You, re-
fulgent as the boulevard sharp
with daylight song, skin, reverie

++++++++++++++++++++++++++++++++++
madness it is, this poem, night
in its untold legend, red black
orange yellow violence, down
the coast in the Wild, moving
pictures silent blank and white,
revealing, You, in the nowhere
with but two hours left to go,
there is no french word for it,
laurel canyon, Calabasas, Ventura
where the insane thrive, finally
to the chapel called Clinging-
to-the-Dead, chimes ring heaven's
knell, small underfoot pansies
pastel mauve and hyacinth like
the first time, you weren't
looking, the deer in the Vedanta
society paddock, pure distance
+++++++++++++++++++++++++++++++
how much gathered in the Lotus,
how little in the heather pink
unfastened in the fog, hillside
in a rush of water, houses long
uninhabited but for the sound
of gravel running through sleep,
You at the top of the stairs?
who is keeping count, who are
the dedicated in the valley,
who the disabled of echo, who
mysteriously return to glass
+++++++++++++++++++++++++++++++
when we get there we can go
to the Chinese theater,
no one will be listening
++++++++++++++++++++++++++++++
will we ever meet, again?
haunting   as beauty
            must be

12-22-06

(conversation)

**it's not the weather, cold, or
the music mid 17th century, again,
the black finger gloves, one inch
and you're in hell, another inch
& one is fit for conversion to a
higher order, red, multiple and
suddenly the dislocation of air,
turbulence like black fire, acid
roses cutting through atmosphere
until do them part, dying, such
as many will never appear again,
so you think to "be" in this clime
untoward, question not the hallowed
fringe that to the brain clings,
fix on the altar the penny weight
denoting as they burn the names,
so when did you begin and what
is it ending, like the time you
forever away had no desire, or
moving from flame to flame, ever
notice the burning moth, ascent
to paradise, fixation for certain
styles of hair, underlying seasons
in stellar combustion, oceans of
light, winds of endless smoke,
will you please quote the price,
brushing away the ash to remain
statue-like, encrustations mosaic
of sound, what is the amazing
thing you're wearing, music?**
++++++++++++++++++++++++++++++++++
**afterwards it becomes weightless,
supposedly like the soul, embrace
me, all around the invisible Fire,**

**month after month it's been now,
what's the talk in heaven, black
limousine and stairs that don't go
all the way, then what's the age
limit for cigarette smokers, why
is the place so dark, who is moving
without shape, why is there no edge,
words fail to maintain discourse,
legend in her enigmatic skin, or
++++++++++++++++++++++++++++++++++
phase of white, followed by blank,
looking for the right "expression",
wearing syntax like illegal arms,
the basic meaning is "elude", grass
swarms the temple, clouds, inky as
Mnemosyne in her see-through shift,
all pale as water on the moon, her
askance as ever glance, though much
traffic floods the afternoon, void,
a regret that cannot be repaired,
once over the larger lens magnifies
the illimitable, a song, Stranger
+++++++++++++++++++++++++++++++++++
lithe as the wind between waists,
the upheld flower blows its colors
into unpromised myth, flings high
a skirt, not what a summer brings,
not what is unspoken, not a sentence
for its variable exultation, am I
done? if this radiance destroys
all night, and though we are
are arrived at noon, in a glass
boat, amid buffeting waves of cinder,
neither to the left nor to the right
sinking the impossible, wingless,
to the sun, where aims a cigarette
its ultimate light, why is it so?
+++++++++++++++++++++++++++++++++++
blown away, look there between
the clouds
you didn't answer**

01-03-07

(stalking)

**it's called "stalking", it's when
a god is mistaken for his automobile,
it's whenever the double strays
from the "other", it's red when
blank should do, whatever it isn't
remains in doubt, cloud work high
because noon is lost, aspirin moon
dissolved in memory's fade, forever
a shift in pale, white as whiter
strewn between the lies that flower,
when hovers between secrets girls
share a darker thought, like air that
fills a sleeping emptiness, like
roses not gathered that in frost die,
a poem "matters", a second glance
reveals the verse of longing loss,
why music undesigned soars in mind
a burning, who ache seeing invisible
the flame that "matters", love's
integer dwells in whom love's integer
fails, how does one make a map of
the world?   out of mists
+++++++++++++++++++++++++++++++++++++
it is coming down from, it is in
deep despair about, it has no more
illusions, going in and out of the
store, looking for what, in search
of, the nevertheless
unfinished   , reaching
for outer space
                                        until
+++++++++++++++++++++++++++++++++++++
so, doesn't matter any more, for why
so much out of place, behind glass,
locked under key, transformed utterly**

banal, switches code fractions
unlimited azure, sky in a single
crease, folded, thrown away
as are all
who sleep
unknowing in mown grass, who under
a spell talk nonsense
assuming neon is heaven,
blank
the innocent, who
++++++++++++++++++++++++++++++++++++++
are there "last times"?
who in a brief episode of light,
somewhere behind a shadow
beckoning,

in a rush
gone

1-30-07

(bedlam : AMOEBA)

great nostalgia for pre-electric era,
what you were doing then, who you were
gathering from gardens wild in bloom
such flowers as a god would choose,
eglantine hyacinth jasmine narcissus,
and a charm would of them make, a
shape of air the size of heaven and
thence make the leap, madness!
to the fourfold paradise down below
to where they make "music" in pairs
of nine, madness what is not remembered,
beyond recall a piece of sky, earth
in dark quarters, You, the however
tender, the nevertheless forgotten,

what myth what arcana, quite the "other"
in your triple bank of red, Hair,
the question of moving forth, of
sending the feathered thought out,
what a shaking down, Madness, beside
the self the extra "being", shades of,
narrow as rivers of, Uranus moving
beyond its dark shelf, Pluto denied,
on the opposite shore in her negligee
of black satin, Echo, cannot hear
++++++++++++++++++++++++++++++++++++++
never said the right thing, quarreled
listening to metal, gunshot in sleep,
each ear attuned to Moon's deep shift,
like a world in rust, ruins wandering
through the archaic, islands forever
adrift in nostalgia of fever, houses,
the uninhabited where you roam still,
legend multiplied by madness, bedlam
aching to Know, forty floors down where
sleepwalkers urge a cigarette, stone
porous and unavailable, Here, I'll give
you a "hand", remember nothing of this,
floating, floating away, foaming, white
++
until all is distance,
walls of fog built on the idea of water,
dialogue with lipstick of longing
"forever"
chain smoking, or
half way down the stairs,
minutiae of breath
Light

1-06-07

(angel face [fragment])

**understand you? "a whole world I lost
for You" it says on the billboard sky
blue, with nowhere to go, angel face
in a crowd, the dense, the intense,
no wonder when it enters a room glows,
a rose in its distance more pales, a
whenever I look the enormous, slays
me with her eyes, are there wings
invisible that assail the gloom, or
heaven on alternate current pulsing
madly, yes, to die in an instant like
"that", who like clouds swarming gaze
for the forgotten, who wandering come
apart, longing, echoes of planets
gone off course plunged into dark,
what does not return, sleep ineffable
features like seraphim, angel face,
herself somewhere aloft, drifting
in and out of music, a smoke riddled
with being, vermillion part in the hair,
like any of Krishna's 3000 brides,
celestial entity, "the" sublime, errant
as water in a dream, Urania, the hush**
++
**melancholy, vast reaches, tundra, lack
of emotion, can it be? angel face regards
the "other", as far as traffic stretches
boulevards of insane "girl" radio, twilit
landscape turning to white dust, overture
to silent seas, moon disrobed, aspirin
color of anxiety, day in and day out, it
will never end, rushes of phlox dogwood
magnolia, phantom turbulence of a missing
heart, who says what the soul "is", who
angel face in proportion to zero, counting
all the spaces in between lives, separate
floral displays for each love, intricacy
going out through grasses, wilderness, a**
+++
perplexed, ambiguities of the archaic,

learning to “desire”, confirming angel face
as the remote, illegible, what is there
to read anyway? who in a desert know at
last there is no Salvation, futility
and burden of the years, what waking
is, what dying can be, slowly lines
ashes mulch powders dissembling “life,”
yellow as fade, red once, night
the alone,
of things
the solitude
immense

01-10-07

(angel baby [fragment])

goddess in a white t-shirt, echoes
nameless across silent, pay for nothing
at the end of the world, pink lipstick
of surprise, then aside whispers to
no one, can it be a “gift”? angel
in disguise speechless, no promises
but the wet shift through darkness,
poetry at two in the afternoon, red
focus, abyss, final things unexpected
as a chinese waterfall on the Avenue,
robbed of music, nothing left but skin
to wear as a song, chimes of hair,
auburn afterthought as locks, clouds
myriad as the fleece of number drifting
through a single Eye, is sleep ideal?
where does it go, looking for whom
at dead end of time, looking for You
in threatening chiffon, icon in slender,
how many ribbons does it take, dream
of “never-ending love”, illusions every

where, walking solitary beach, homeric,
adrift   shadow, whispers
++++++++++++++++++++++++++++++++++++
minute drops, grey drizzle afternoon
hurrying through glass, opaque, vision
caught on the swinging door, a face
lifted seraphic blank, more pale as
angel baby longs, what is lost, what
will never be understood, in rags of
light, shafts of energy devour meat,
mind alters its flame, house consumed
+++++++++++++++++++++++++++++++++++++++
why it is so, white unobservable, blue
dispatched by cherubim into the void,
yellow withering, like evening star
dissolved in aspirin, empty,
vast
(every time I see you, angel baby,
the decorations are different
breath is a tight fit
I become tongue-tied
at a loss for Sounds)
who are "we"
if not in the hereafter
"echoes"

01-13-07

[waterfall on mount lu]
For Maurice Weddington

what strangers in mists their
shadows lose a distance no less
some fragments a spray for whom
no love fell this story sends
her must be the rust of swoons
some weary soul his body bent
no longer but to some dream inn

wends his ancient carcass spent
will then such travelers mind
a crevice stony steep for sleep
a harsh late winter rends this
falling water out of the sky
this matted cloud light undone
a hand this brushed ink delight
once breathed a shape fantastic
on this silk raveled score like
music real & sacred binding us
to cliffs unearthly heavens
and have no more but to walk
away in fogs silently rolling
where is no trace but longing
some far gone hoary myth
out of time a mountain drawn

(based on the painting by Sheng Maoye,
1625-1640, Ming Dynasty)

03-30-07

[Lucretius to his Venus]

the world around me begins to swim
in the inky maelstrom of self-delusion
to nothing nothing goes all blank
pages the sterility of no conclusion
whitens matters left undone the last
a letter flung from the whorled maze
a sound in dreams confused by time
a lone the thing that sings unstrung
like planets nameless in the void
how do we come this way back?
is a memory a likeness to the One
or are all oceans in the single drop
a vast unfounded intellect gone mad?
is to the left the right handed Bride

the palest shade gone dumb
how deeply flowers in their little
scope the width of space endure
this scent past dying spreads around
like light shed myriads of eons hence
shall I Thee number amongst the few
who crown the angelic mount?
or fail I to recall that even once
you fled and fell among ferny green
a wing a lip a moan in the dappled gyre
is each the other flown a whitened
shire among chapels blasted out
or does the air yet hum a distant spring
a lattice work behung with silent bells
a poem in evidence of the grassy Step
do under then we go in the briny sweep
who weep in dreams of ancient Dust
alas the

fragments the archaic hold
such a sweetness in the bower
does each leaf your Name implore
does each blade a tongue conspire
who burns the every word
were earth not such a dolorous thing
this enigma this sleep
do none then escape this sphere
this sentence of unremembered Flame?

(05-02-07)

[canto]

who are coming to an end, this end,
who are speaking the last word, who
cannot recall how to say it, this last
word, what word, moving a stone from

this place to there, cutting a rock,
rock crystal hewn, why I am remembering
these things, do not ask why, who I am
forgetting, what pleasure it was invoking
what, who in rooms apart or lightless
witnessing the dark, sleeping matters
as much as the windows they lack, who
to repeat, who are drawing from the shore
shapeless boats, nets in which a small
god drowned revives, to die again, soul
pierced through by a needle, myth of
regrets, sewn to the eyelid so the dream
cannot end, who lay down the body, who
strewn across an infinite beach count
the mind's flames, endless as the seven
heavens of paradise, endless as the stone
being moved back from there to here, crystal
in the eye, a small gold fleck buried in
the ear, flashes in the brain's conjecture
to realize, I am as much as that single
"flash", waking as if an "other", to whom
address these syllables, of burning, inchoate
sound like a sea being born or not ending,
++
there will not be so much now, even less
unwinding within the only number, stars are
insane switching on and off, planets emptied
of all content aim for destruct, who is in mind
if not the burnt corpse, if not the house
without walls, who are taking down one by one
the letters of a secret alphabet, mornings
seared by what remains, who have asked for
a life and receive a night in the desert,
alone, as for that matter who is not, athirst
for the unknown, for what cannot be remembered
++
who in the poem recite verses of disintegration,
who circle endlessly, listening to a voice
without translation, idiocy of being, immanence
of a celestial absence, the insane chance to
breathe walking among angels dead, long after
thought of them has been removed, a stone at

**a time, moving shadows as if they were weight,
heaving into the pool this inkling, this small
"thing", I am neither as before or as of now,
neither here nor where there was a tale, ash**

05-19-07

(Hare Krishna)

*"in the whole world there is only one man: Krishna.
Everyone else is a woman" (Mira Bai)*

**if I'm not Madonna, who is? says a long time ago
suing for air time in a question of doubt, former
white pale blank blanch fade where nothing really
all colors at a loss or no color at all, was red
when now the stripe in vermillion electrifies who
buys this or that hoping for the unheard Note,
imagine as if, falling from grace into a language
when nothing can happen, sleeping in the undertow
wasting away, the nuisance of being, peach flavored
indigo clouds withering the horizon, dreams are
in conjunction, the highest peak can never be,
just like the time your face manifested on the
marble floor in the drug store, sex like ice-cream
in the illusion that it will last, a focus dark
as spirits are in the future, what is impossible
or madness revolving around the single iris, amaze
++
dancing, tom-tom beat, crazy and irreverent statue
whose feet are painted the color of narcissi
whose hands bear stigmata of the blessed lord
whose face is a derangement of holy emotions
whose whatever you want to call it
it starts where it ends, as always, a function
of the orgasm, pulling the sky out of shape
with massive electrical discharge, streaks**

across the painted window, exhausted and freaky
listening for the little radio to open up
a music   shifts in time, emptiness
at the heart of it all
waiting forever in the airport at the end
of the world   ominous roar of surf
night   chaos, demons
++
wherever I will be, you too
if ever I am, you too
whoever I can never be, you too
it isn't every day this happens, for you too
this is the moment I become other, a book at
a time, page after page burning, you too,
flames that devour the heart, the mind, flames
the house catches
whatever is not smoke is
why didn't you write like you promised
why didn't you
               my head aches, supernal one
falling out of one heaven into the next,
falling from paradise
automobiles are moving in the other direction
there is no one around, a vacuum
like watching the movie you promised me
somewhere, somehow
                    holding hands,
wearing your hair, wearing your lingerie
breathing   , breathing

06-07-07

(what a poem means)

if it isn't in red written all
over the white side of invisible
ink and the envelope folded neatly

in thirds like the time you were
crossing from devil to angel not
looking for the traffic's direction
words evaded you in the ambulance of
loving the next thing to a body
or a siren whip-lashed to a mast
with meat stuck in the ears for not
hearing so beautiful was the rapture
sublime disorientation emotionally
dead as you were waves raging tossed
into the glass unable to drown but
heaven spent in the myth of your Eye
floral games in maze cerulean saffron
dizzy headlong plunge into midst
where all Noon occurs as "the" cipher
until nothing else matters nor does
Shiva dominant in his wild dance
care for this is the no thing the
++++++++++++++++++++++++++++++++++++
then what is written does not happen
in the reader's absence of night
space at full tilt in the broadside
the ancient ceremony of memory yellow
as the rushing grasses of fading time

[otherwise]

secrets in the grass, once over
who remembers what the poem was
reading slowly in clouds evening
color of silence and distance
going to bed with the Other a
finite body Eros, legend has
a different shadow today a more
elegant composure beneath the
why did you never tell me Why?
empty mirror and behind it land

no one has ever seen before
each takes a step into the water
what is not known, to suffer
consciousness
a hymn rises from the brushes
russet and saffron gorgeous music
wordless beside the engraved stone
that is a tomb, fingers weave
night's immense but fragile skin
I am dreaming
white intaglios
of thought proceeding
from out of the inextricable green
a warning or confusion of angels
some blind behind metal
others simply being,
or not
everything is forgetting
ultimately the island we were meant
to visit itself lifts into the fire
which eternalizes itself
+++++++++++++++++++++++++++++++++++++
impermanence, who
and by chance are waiting
on the other side
not the same as before
but not otherwise
so do not hurry
the City
built ten times upon itself
is only sleeping,
the rest is darkness
leaf balcony and memory

09-03-08

MADONNA AT FIFTY: REREADING MADONNA

**the poet as conjecture at a point
probably a maniac totally outside
the self, the so called, Self
propelled by ambiguity of sex
and alienation into vast cavity
oneiric indulgence in Isla Bonita
dancing with an empty blond hat
beyond the gulf of sanity and death
into surfeit of suburban violence
beyond his or anyone's control
"you're an Angel" et and cetera
and et Fucking cetera (Lamantia
dead now two years?) incense polluted
cathedral, is it anger? is it sulphur?
is it Hotel nirvana? what is it?
just what kind of problems do Americans
have today? indigenous people's Act
annul All treaties and in hell everyone
doing lip synch to Lowell Fulson's
"Like a Baby" breathless over death valley
where Big yucca tree points to quadrant
in sky where syntax turns into saffron
eating first the Lips then the Heart
then whatever else Tokyo Manga rose
can deliver it better for less shopping
like a girl for leftovers in parking
lot malt liquor overdose, it is
least of all a poem but a Vision
Blake with his lambs and seraphim
in wraparound Roy Orbison shades Oh
what quantity of boulevard speeding
straight into Natalie Wood's watery
graveyard and matchless for her skin
the endless be-alike of Girl in Question
revolving like a Trionfo della Morte
on her pedestal Renaissance in bright
flake twill Thee for whom I sing ad
Nauseam!   like ten years later
and still limping from aggregate of**

horrors in orangery far from center
of home fearing the double lurking behind
hollywood hills with neon dagger &
ciceronian lisp fakes amoeba Musick fiend
like the mornings I'd rush to the computer
to punch all the adjacent syllables
rendering a 17th century sonata Dead
for all to hear toneless in arcadia
wasn't that what I wanted? to destroy
virtually all sense of linearity and Form
there is no purgatory only meaningless
moral turpitude in hospital for the
dead-ended like Orlando in search
of his wit-cup on the Moon, what sheer
Lunacy depraved going in circles rutting
after Angelica the untouchable in her
tunnel of moors and dacoits
+++
to think "it could never end"
to think that step after step only the
cliff remained Only the Lonely haunted
by Unchained Melody rummaging for auto
parts in cemetery rust memorabilia
or some desolate freeway to San Bernardino
driven in a car by brainless Pachucos
who think Led Zeppelin is a King
the whole and entire inordinate sense
of nothingness of it all for Christ's
bloody Sake reciting to a wall covered
with pinups in stages of undress monologue
of virtue annihilated, can it be far?
++
what has started as an itch an obsession
a mania a compulsion a stalker in stiletto
heels with a mind bent on camera eye seduction
until in the back seat at fever pitch
listening to the only song there is
Frozen ad infinitum as they say in Paradiso
dancing with the drowned the damned the
irresolute of attention with a minute
cut on the rump a small bruise near
the medulla where it says in bright

red ink I am the Way who can suffer
countless the errors of the imagination
"you're kidding" buying at a remainder sale
the big poster photo of Her in what's left
of reality a skimpy hitch-hiker's dream
who restless to have more cannot find It
who will even trade sex for a brief half
the section just under age by Sepulveda Blvd
who are running tongues hanging out
after the motorcade that bears the Corpse
the heavenly One out of range
into what bric a brac of post modernism
daydreaming that emerging from the Surf
botticelli's Venus will assume the Light
taking from heaven the motionless stars
who and who else but the poets
to eat or discard as style demands
her stepping on burning sand as if
or removing the shell from her Pubis
reveals at last the
ancient the archaic Homeric hexameter
dragging around the walls of troy
for her sake lifeless Hector
forgetting to lock the door after her
leaving pools of salt water and bracken
oblivious to the day that generated her
and the syntactic derangement of Mind
staggered and staring into broken glass
the myriad refractions and pointillism
each as the One involving itself
with the Self!   madness and dereliction
auto-destruct the shaved idea of Time
from which nothing proceeds
the poet as conjecture
the   unfinished

8-15-08

(LIVING GODDESS) KUMARI

**finite and preadolescent maoist come
to terms paint the Face melting ochre
and yellow hint of hyacinth jasmine
mountain mist off the faded brick
how much noise in such a little Ear
how much less the divine in a cell-phone
played back the compact priestly Fix
himalayan mysteries remote interiors
durga Puja forced to drink alcohol
until tongue a blur and shocked Eye
revolves OM darkens archaic and hush
who will not come of age because History
torn from roof of mouth incandescent
compiling pages of cloth fluttering
from top of World buddhists born
in the body of a Hindu goddess dancing
on red in all its carmine vermilion
Blank receding shades if it is night
ages pass of kings and armies rushing
silver to its moon of silent Light
bangles copper tone anklets shimmering
plate of skin turning color of afternoon
or sleeping like leaf bound in coral
can sometimes matter the inch of flesh
paraded in saffron canopy of endless paper
to burn as symbols required of language
who will take hair making it Big black
as the ingot of a dream gold is having
but cannot return Girl whose other face
in glass beads perspires planets rung
chimes in brassy quills high as cloud
shaping Self into changeless breath**

08-18-08

[at Delphi]

**numbed by what passes for tragedy
on the Autobahn, no one shares
no one confides mortgage confirmation
but for Girlfriend manifested
from dreamstuff oriental and red
haunting life's end with tantalizing
swimming through sleep a haunt
who can recover from this penalty?
as if waking to another world
is memory a decay of senses or
passing like dumb angels through
maelstrom of ambiguity I will
keep nothing at hand, dying is
a next passage wherein read "sublime"
voices heighten outside the glass
who gather shadows to ruminate
where something else ends, question
dense like the trilogy of hair
worn by the first bride in devotion
turning toward the flame her face
fane of infirm signs to embroider
the poem in its disparity, a will
hers is the edge the fire within
devouring all substance is why
I cannot recall well the Wedding,
metropolis of hidden intentions
++++++++++++++++++++++++++++++++++++
what sudden whim the shepherd displays
his oaten reed a melody descries
am I wont to hear from afar a water
meandering through unbidden wall?
consigned to eternity mind's cloudy
form dissolves its one slow thought
alas we who thought to Know
can see no more love's indentation
nor from where we stand on perilous
stage discern which planet now
consumes itself in fiery enterprise**

09-21-08

(FRANK O'HARA)

imagine finding you on the second floor of
Moe's in Berkeley 21st century
not like the Buddha preaching in Essen
nor like the "encounter" in Grand Central
but full impeccably of Nostalgia
was art ever so supremely modern?
nor are the fiery triptychs of memory
any more discernible than clouds
the ultimately many the scattered
the massively random with their tiny moons
that clutter the everyday head
can it be Noon on your side of paradise
longing as the Japanese do for an
arcadia of blank but massive walls rearing
their concrete muscles into the orangery
of a sky long since abandoned by the Tao
Frank! decades have passed since your
stupid Death and none are the wiser for it
but continue to practice a poetry of sorts
without the city of intricate dreams you
employed lunching with angels in traffic
and jack hammers and pornographic art shoppes
how unwholesome the trade of lyrics is
the shameful quotidian of willfully ignoring
when beauty has but to shove an index
finger into the Iota of their thoughtlessness
and to point brightly to the sun really
unabashed on its pointillistic horizon like
Dawn such as it happened to you repeatedly
elegant in trousers flaming like Mayakovski
or for that matter Lorca in his Nueva Yorque
of albino lovers and sudden surrealism
in the Cedar Tavern or Uptown with the art
people drunk and nibbling on Hans Arp cheese

can it for that matter be so different today
the buzz of wireless cell phone conversation
or the immediate fall of the Dow ten thousand
points a minute until somewhere below nadir
Lady Murasaki takes you by the lapels
and shakes you awake from silken drowsiness
forgetting how to use the Honorific pronoun
because in you the Urgent is at once Distance
and the ever unfulfilled last poem
written on the back of a napkin before lipstick
was invented or darkness inside a phone booth

10-06-08

INCOMPLETE CANTO
FOR ANNO DOMINI 2009

what's the relationship between
bleach and blanch
and for that matter Blank
as in "blanche-fleur"
you was my bride in XXth century
furiously et cetera
goddamned how the troubadours
and the Etruscans on their shiny lake
a cargo of five hundred thousand
ducats and wearing velvet foolscap
the emergent picture is one of
ignorance drunken self-pity
"lussuria" jazz in the wrong hour
of days without memory sloth
in basements waking to sharp light
of conscience and dreary text
latin latin and more latin
catullus but not propertius
lucretius splitting the atom

**near the corner of ellis and 59th
Bo Diddly the self made guitar
which it is being a Man
junction of time and space
“high” on roof top abracadabra
or that are perhaps fractions
from an ancient poesy “tying
her hair in a topknot” for a
divinity to manifest by the
and moreover the wellsprings
of sorrow ingratitude mockery
not understanding rightly the
Nature of things viz-a-viz
lucretius “antichissime mura”
undoing her girdle in the middle
because of the extreme heat
as lurid the pictures turn round
and round hands gritty soiled
from pornography and juxtaposed
the Seder waiting for the Stranger
anomalous pages torn from classics
to illustrate beneath the buttocks
a pillow in length the size of
memory itself agony and dreamed
over and over the divorce
papers signed in a dickensian
bureau shafts of ill-gotten
fire distributed among the heroes
philistines (i.e. Palestinians)
hauling ashore the alphabet triremes
sweating in sandstorms eating
leftovers of pig dog urine slop
who can but explain this plight
agony blinded at the millstone
in gaza question mark mysteriously
posited in her ovaries
the bunch of keys her hair her
ink-stained school books ABC
of love in 12th century ingots
plastered the junk shoved into a
just sat there staring for hours
darkness of history**

++

"weaving the garments of the deities"
how sweet   matter
the great greensward beneath
bunches of phlox   fled
into the willow grove her feet
naked   to read there
bucolics of Theocritus while
in the future wars rage
ponds fill with blood bile gore
heavens gape   nuisance
to be alive amid rubble groping
here there was a
the letters no longer make sense
in the apartment a complete hush
waiting for   rockets
hissing   who once prayed
in the grass extended their shadows
love-making
whole afternoons consumed
in the skin read the literature
of sweat while bees knit
their intricate orient of sound
in the sleeper's Ear

will we ever be allowed back?

01-11-09

[elegy for joel pugh]
for james balfour

a lifetime, disappeared
into which quarter of the sky
the chinese invented fabulous
celestial entities powder rockets
shining other things, loosely

**involved the skin undoing by one
after another the desires
looking no more for the Cave
or else getting by
mirrored in a water far away
longing, called echo by a
different name with brightly
colored skirts a paradigm of
youth like a metal in summer
hot seemingly indestructible
until one day writing backwards
come to terms with, on lawns
of evening fade the chill
of alcohol and girlfriends
who come to be in the telephone
a section of cloud limited
to memory only the rest being
an acquired "second" language
a poem, perhaps, elegiac
running the fingers over a surface
which is music or night or
because there is no word for it
who are shouting into the wall
pulverized, I am definitely
this small organism called sleep
this portion of shadow that
clings to the enormous green outside
when water suddenly manifests
with its myriad faces of myth
drowning, a lifetime
is,**

01-14-09

[darkness gathering, the]

"l'édifice immense du souvenir"
m. proust

not otherwise, for the moment the slender
blades a radiance, can it be sleeping?
imagine the massive subterfuge to be
nothing but air, or its absence, remember
nothing at all but for her passing
naked through the night, then echo's
small and plangent grass by the window
where a god forgetful of his dress
waits for the planet, plunging
through a water so immense that
whoever said it could be kenned
listening, you were almost "there"
for a whole summer maybe becoming green
silent emerging outside the fragile
shell of the self, who arbitrary
and cruel ascertained that distance was
the dominant mode, the music of madness
sounding a little metal, because,
shifts from white pale merely sheen
invisible really or blending into
the bright cloth, other side of what?
expecting to be served a childhood
in a mansion carved out of sand until
all of space, a clock ticking red
within the Ear, "I am orestes" said
repeatedly to the whirring maenads
who are come to the Hill, take me
all the thing is broken
++++++++++++++++++++++++++++++++++++
after all these years a century
poised like a droplet on the edge
a moon dissolving in the morning's
one instant of oblivion, who will
change masks slowly going from room
to room glass in hand, asked to leave
the company of strangers, alone
for what seems

you are urged to age, to lessen
the maximum security which life is
outside where a weather darkens
it is afternoon gathering
a language lesson, pronouns remote
and honorific none of which apply
you are becoming ineffable
a pointillistic backdrop
to an already impalpable montage
the excuse is worn, nobody
believes you were ever
here
can hear the immense scaffolding
coming apart in the dream
like sections of her name
you can no longer recognize “it”
what stands
what falls
the unhealed wound
how long ago that was
until death do us
++++++++++++++++++++++++++++++++++++

the middle is become the end

(for jack foley)

01-23-09

(“the” secret poem)

because can never, be, reveal
nothing despite rain and forecast
cloudy, how as many the years
rolled thunder in loose heads
margined by beauty’s self,
illusion, to exchange one book

**for the map of skin and the,
other, for what has never been,
who will look askance at limitless
the sea, immense below sky equally
immense and, wounded, equivocation,
fault line zooming toward orient
to poetry's flawed mansion, how
many housed in tiers of animal
and magnet, her face, Her eyes!
flashing iridescence & excitement
(does age matter?), this ancient
thought this manifest of eld, whose
and for what shapes green manifold
garden swarms luscious love's again-
bite until, Dreamer! riot in the
welkin, planets aflame, puzzled page
the enigma of Minerva stalking
grasses of sleep, shakes the hand
this inch of desire in what map,
longing for the, has ever sought
ages in the Eye, what hear the Muses
then in their grotto, I am to her
what marble is to the mind, she is
to me, what, Ear, music contained
the unfurled in peals of rose and
ash, how much a horizon, how little
sea-bottom, deaf as a moon unseen,
cannot dare to Touch, following
the thread of her passage crimson,
at first, then whittled to a small
magenta, red involving, trying to
read editions azure, how far
distance extends into its Space,
initials in dissolved ink, nebula,
fossil, shifting, bone, cold,
the interior of History, causeless
her voice, Singing!**

02-22-09

(the "next" secret poem)

**which is not revealed, neither for
her depth which is like the floor
a bottomless, dreaming once that I
was reaching for the celestial, a,
shadow more like speed than light
running across the blaze of hair
itself black satin, who calls out
from the air that nothing remains,
that from the precipice we call life
a formidable ruin wavers, oblique,
fastened to only the color green
from the waist down, fluid as hotels
so extensive they cannot exist,
sectioned like a poem is for mystery
enigma the archaic and arcane, Muse,
no fixity in memory fluid antinomies
that are not days, mars, mercury, et
cetera divided into distances of remote,
at the apex a residue of planet ochre
burnt rust rushes, trying to hear what
it said in passing, grasses, swiftness
of feet becoming ice, as ancient as
dust burning at the center of things,
when we can no longer "become" but
remain as the static that reaches across
the immense beyond of the Ear, whispers,
the taint of nothingness, her, a syllable,
dashed against the grain like spit, a,**

02-23-09

[a small poem about]

**of all the lives, a life, this
one, air of sky & clouds of in-
transigence, walking as if to discover
or uncover an afternoon, in Love
with the idea, or else nothing matters,
flowers white dogwood magnolia
oleander phlox snowballs Your face
among the flora sleeping, what
green sap runs through yr veins
what tributary of blood exclaims!
seeing you is to know everything,
then oblivion, hell the thorny Hades
of Achilles, wound is eternal as
is the poetry of it, darkness
going down from the house of Light
into the miserable basement, how
can it be recovered that moment
when brimming with life you ran
from course to course to Understand
what little, sometimes the intense
blue is Too much, we waver as if
nothing to hold, the size of it is
what cannot be explained, you will
be gone in a matter of minutes a
shadow fled off the floor, ghost
a fragment of
            to remember**

03-27-09

"summer ghosts"

things gossamer like water sleep
shimmering silvery drowned already
these few centuries was it alive
a rumor murmuring shadows dreamt
occasion of glass reflections dead
a silhouette against book-spines
everything fluid heat distances
even voices rumpled weary indistinct
over waves leaden carrying ghosts
toward what tenement fire leaves
for sifting ashes hands unnumbered
like rivers cinder-colored oriented
in flush aspersions clouds heaving
roof against roof cataclysmically
dormant big-bang ear drilled OM
shading leftwards sump slumbered
flesh driven mechanically bereft
souls in long division amazed what!
southern horizon ice melting slow
dancing hip shaped darkness limbo
frayed brushwork tinged inky velvet
eye-pupils fingered illusion sighted
avenues secretly named after girls
undressed sheets sweating lingered
telling fabulous memories tongues
hair waist abandoned sex wetness
drained each center pitted black
oblivion's ruddy inch pacing hard
sky's last hour thundering long
afternoons brick by brick undone
yellow passion fading faint pallid
echoes whispering hushed silence
wondering who and if ever again

07-19-09

(poem)

chinese waterfalls
behind veils of mist
in a landscape painting
are more real than this

not men, shadows

07-04-10

"to die"

it's what's left to do
you dry your eye
distance is beyond
everything imaginable
roll yourself up in dust
blank each thought
until there is no pattern
yellow descends into night
white silence immobility
skin loses itself at last
in water shadowless
infinite in depth
dream dissolved
sky cloud light
the going out
going out
out

7-24-10

"a dream"

(i)

skeleton of two trees black
on a winter hill

the pond below reflects
nothing back

when you read this
if you will read this

think of me somewhere
between space & time

(ii)

long hot afternoons
of a forgotten summer
gone

(breath , light ,
the insubstantial)

07-28-10

"It's all about death"

eyes like emerald clouds
the first dance perfume dark
abyss in a whirl lipstick
chance kiss behind white
and night windowless
and infinite beyond lasting
stars like fireflies in the brain
dizzy inch of meat stained
portion of hematite softening

into dream of girls waterswept
ageless as Ophelia

10-17-10

"beowulf"

in god-mead drowned sings song
bard of baleful harp-notes heard
oh th'unruly heart's found flung
thus thrust sword's swerving side
into depths thoughtlessly thrown
no mere man's mind muddied
but e'er shines day's glow-sheen
anon through death's meadow drear

10-27-10

"calaveras"

insignificant day
even of the dead a
painted skull positioned
at the small entrance to hell
just a few feet away
from the circulation desk
in what seems to be a state
of tension garlanded
with a scarf over the head
of an erstwhile student
a novice at color or
what performs as shape and

substantially disoriented
a few hours and the Past
resurrects its inch
of immemorial flame
turning to ash the mill
of desire and flotation
++++++++++++++++++++++++
in a year or less
insignificant as the dead
may seem in their wreaths
oblivion discharges its
might across the darkening
waters of when nothing
matters to come back
dreams spilled like ink
untranslatable over
the now indistinct Page
when neither You
nameless in your modernity
nor I the ancient bonze
have hands to exchange
nor lips to endeavor
+++++++++++++++++++++++++
wraiths shadows truncated
by the Hour flimflam discourse
so much being said
but nothing being pronounced
stone and nostalgia
impenetrable as night's
unending rationale
a few notes of song
bone-text the archaic
distance the All
silence and more
silence

10-20-10

"beyond the reach of memory"

**it was only last night
a hundred billion trillion
Light Years and eons more
than what my Eye perceived
was I aloft in the dark cradle
beyond the reach of memory
spent of breath released
from meat's feverish itch
driving and driven through
the massive and intricate syntax
of light a glaze of antiquity
of sands without reckoning
a pyramid of thought and
all was loss!
adrift without words a sleep
lavender silk ropes slipped
from mortal grip the bulk
of Time less than the weight
of dew evaporating in dream
beyond the reach of memory
afloat in the vast of the Void
passing and being passed
through the wilderness of the Dead
after which there is naught
but the poetry of soundlessness**
++++++++++++++++++++++++++++++++
**shall I erect the steeple?
shall the denizens of the other
time re enter this moment
when life itself becomes the
other in a mirror of absent forms?
beyond the reach of memory
nestled in the bank of Space
where inch after inch topples
a water of beautiful decay
until what remains is the Planet
of unknown birth and
but why go on?
come crashing in the single Ear
the green the red the folded blank**

the endless ennui of yellow
the derelict splendor of violet
all the wonders of Sight
when to the blind no anchor
avails and to the deaf
shot through a lightning bolt
an ampersand settles accounts
with the glazier's pallid frost
+++++++++++++++++++++++++++++++++
will You go with me then
beyond the reach of memory?
will you set your unfelt foot
down where nothing ever was?
will you surrender simply
what you never owned
what never you could describe?
will You?
beyond the reach of memory
realm of shifting nameless Cloud

        where nothing ever was

11-23-10

"brilliant"

brilliant is a phase
        is a "face"
this morning as on no other
sun fractures glass high
tones revolve circumflex
accent on the invisible the
One who mysteriously entwined
in knots of air inclined red
the fierce sun itself an "other"
beyond any planetary legend
if it had a name

if it wore something besides
the enigmatic nonchalance
of a smile meant for the deity
of small change of small talk
for the divinity inherent
in skin the implausible the
uniquely like You!
it is outside where your "being"
is an inference of leaf & grass
the shadow asleep in the sky
whose soundless endlessness
assumes a cloud of indifference
the white adagio of dream
a music of spheres of Light
rounding the final autumn
of the Empyrean until
the muse Mnemosyne herself
rising from a vat of water
shakes her massive hair
unwinding immense poetries:
Brilliant as the foam of the Eye
Brilliant as the rose of the Eye
Brilliant as the moon of the Eye
Brilliant as the seas of the Eye
Brilliant as the dust of the Eye
never fading
the fire in the back of the Brain!

in the imminent destruction
of Time
spreading
in ever greater whorls of spent
star surf

into the B E Y O N D
"end of the world"

THE THREE MADONNAS

"there is a light above my head
into your eyes my face remains"
(Paradise not for me)

ANOTHER MADONNA (POEM)

I don't know what is it the rain
the "you're still the same" song
about others the dangerous line
between past and pluperfect a dense
how your eyes drift out of the swarm
lending to the dark a real allure
a shining aren't you even when
night casts about for a star a single
one instead of this afterglow this
impenitent chasing after You reading
in books the phrases that least
define you alter ego plasma jet stream
decadent aloof stinging musically
dead the atrophied of photograph
and sound recording digitized to
resemble the girl in the alley
the tramp the frump the wanton the
you name it jade slut hoyden Blazes!
now into your sixth decade pallid
lips cream colored designer breasts
and hips in the saddle for no one
does tissue regenerate? a hoax a
dream inside a movie about a dream
language filtered through a prism
of Venetian blinds slatted and hoisted
knickered out of control jazzed blue
whatever innocence was in the lurid
detail about where you first did what
to the besotted deity who framed

you in technicolor virtuality a coke
bottle for simulation driving around
empty parking lots looking for the
pepperican kid with Spanish fly Blazes!
a situationist lexicon for deviance
and cosmetic refractions about Chaos
the lingering boom which is a whisper
in the art galleries where imitations
of You crawl in search of the Hit
absinth colored brain and tripe and suet
for lunch the hero on a platter stiff
with the negatives of your out-take
in the cinema reduct below the entrance
to Hades where the other kid Achilles
stoned on angel dust waits gibbering
for your arrival already Hours late
if not centuries in an ambulance
known as the Vatican Whore steamy
revelations of an epidermic cycle
featuring Orlando and Angelica be-bopped
to death on a lunar berlitz tour
so how can You! ancient as Petronius
this rain unabated has one thought
only your Skin the song about a
all the windows are frozen like your
heart in a radical symmetry for an Eye
syntax won't hold and all the waters
of just go down the pandemonium
where poets of echo strangle each other
Oh be Real! instead of this downloaded
printout of you aetas twenty-Nothing!

06-28-11

(MORE) MADONNA POEM

**OK so it was a rant a zen clip
fogbound in your bright red kimono
backdrop of inkblack night trans-
mogrified for all eternity
am I willing? aching for centuries
now the waves' incessant roar
in the tiny crepuscular Ear
brings back what song what meter
that look of absolute defiance
isn't this a sort of madness?
isn't this over the top, Angel Baby?
revisit the haunts where most you meant
to me the accident of infinity
the fragrance of a wreck for all time
cheap pizza and piña colada
mugging among the dead adolescents
in their manicured rags and pot
"darkening in the depths" freight
of floral decadence lace ruptured
panty hose and fruit laden brassiere
un hunh Honey hold on it's universe
deflect our own individual Silence
in order to revolutionize Beauty!
on the ocean bound boulevards
car radios go Whammo! self indulgent
lyric "bad romance" over and over
vertigo stare the apocalyptic
in all this din where is the
strategic Echo? Eurydice? Dido?
"remember me but forget my fate"
hunh? it wants to be gorgeous
it wants to be ineffably sweet
it wants to be whatever You want to be!
I can never be That (vedic tautology)
I can never be You never be You
chiesa della Gran Madre camposanto
baffling   angry   passionate
shall I meet You then on the banks
of the Phlegethon errant souls flitting
shall I grace Thee then with sprays**

**of laurel dogwood and eglantine?
hard by the stony cleft a Voice
emerges mysteriously unintelligible
'twas the Sybil of Cumae speaking
from out of rock crystal hoar
it wants to practice dead But
I am only in paradise sleeping
with your photograph next to me
"my Nenuphar we are never to be joined"
I am ever in Hell waking
with your photograph next to me
who will punctuate the last paragraph?
who will enervate the Judge?
it is the syntax of the Eye
it is beside the Self an Other
it is below the margin of right thinking
parallel madnesses one for the Soul
and the other for its Twin
who can never be You never be You
not even wearing your castoffs
strutting before the mirror of unconscious
who can never be unless it is stoned
hematite and verdigris shoes
walking all over me the hundred times
how came we to this junction?
listening and waiting on a strand
in far off Sri Lanka where Hanuman
staggers high on Bang his eyes
the eyes of Sita! his mouth
the mouth of Sita! who then am I?**

06-29-11

EXTRA MADONNA (POEM)

**it's the end of history and I feel
dirty about it the gloss worn off
the skin a twilit tarnish hue weary
scales come off vision and ears leak
a hissing rasp at the fundament
illusory girls on a romp in black
and white rewind reround film loop
so to sleep again where the Other
has fallen off in the mangrove plot
far from the birthstone farther
still from the hyssop and jasmine
that decked her recolored hair black
this time in the japanese manner
"nothing really matters" shaking
an admonitory finger at me! who
should know better in the labyrinth
of self deceit recoiling in fogs
and antinomy distant as that is
from the franco-italian magazines
endorsed by her lipstick thumbed through
worn at the dog defiled in stalls
too dark to remember who and where
end of history a chapter in microform
regression to a water as enormous
as ink and turning yellow fronds frayed
around mythical edges where no page
can take shape drowned world skin
"the voice of Virgil" descending
like a bass chord running figures
of baroque and abstract elegance
filigrees of pompadour and shadow tint
chiaroscuro behind the lines of her face
held up through time by photographic
process talking to no particular window
at the time of day when the sun
hearkens to Calypso to draw in the nets
straining to hear let alone remember
that song "if I could melt your heart"
ending the various calendar threads
and chronologies making no more sense**

**than a dream I am having or not having
listing from top to back the various
rigamarole and vogue fandango elicited
for some pornographic stunt in latin
she is neatly inserted into the text
rump first until the emperor Domitian
faints from desire all white breaks
out slim stemmed roses burst fantastic
the gesso Christ just melts in her lap
I am having no recall the last day of
history the element of Doubt painted Red
large on the elastic screen of Time
there now you have it misunderstood
verbatim disillusionment Thank You!
look to the clouds forming in the upper
quadrant of the vespers della Beata Vergine
longing echoes of horn and conch
it will be later in the Ganges a chant
for the dead for the untimely dead for
whatever else you may call it Her is
a strumpet in the key of Delta a moist
subterfuge in the brain circling its
own self unremunerated and exhausted
dipped into a vat of abstract expressionism
until there is none left drained of
fading a phantogram of memory
some small letters like a
shaping grass or dew
where none have walked
timeless the enigma
ineffable
dark**

6-29-11

(muse)

bewitches men with her hair
flame red apostolic ruin of a text
going everywhere at once
like the Prophet in the tavern
in everyone's eyes but Nowhere
in sight a riot of color in a place
called the World unexamined
entering Etruscan country
near the gateway to Hades
but nothing seems to be what
air clouds azure stippled a gate
forms out of water and foot-
steps her on the run hidden
skin foliage of lissome her
waist and hips dangerously
white anxiety is like that a
fixation of night wakes a
startled anemone of red light
crashing silently through space
her mind at work inside yours
shape of words without meaning
syllables from pine and reed
swaying a wind yellow soft
trestles rattling because dark
withers the glass into sand
sand into burrows of light
light into expanses of moon
nothing lasts it all goes away
even sleep with its thirty knots
undone like her tresses dissolves
into the fundament where stars
like crickets in a chinese painting
create then destroy their flickering
misunderstood by men who
waking decide to hunt & conquer
but not you Poet undecided wary
not sure what her Name is
or could be listening only to
the lapping of water in a distance
you can only assume is there before

falling back into the dream about
the face your mother gave you
++++++++++++++++++++++++
each is certainly the Other
she appears disappears rattles
a gourd shakes leaves from a bough
taunts you sticks her tongue out
rolls her eyes back curses you
with a snap of her fingers
exhausts you with shadow play
so intricate you surrender
not sure to what thinking Yes
it is a poem this handful of gravel
that you toss as if casting lots
into the small dimension of life
reappears behind you this time
singing as if to never end
that celestial melody of madness
pulls you by the hair bites your
ear casts you down dancing
on your spine with her rhythm
like a juggernaut rolling weightless
over the extension of your ego
until you are become the Nothing
the cipher inside the zero
the edgeless unfathomed
the ink the size of Time
++++++++++++++++++++++
do not bother to come back
not to this not to the writing
on the margins not to the story
which has been left untold
do not try to make sense
it is a mystery a bell tolling
where there is no sound
it is an enigma how she
weaves in and out unseen
leaving everywhere her Mark
the indelible syllable
to repeat which makes you crazy
you ken nothing of it
it is beyond you

**mere pattern of light
in the senseless array
without beginning or end
the engine of her Heart
the
a flame
D I O T I M A
(for neeli cherkovski)**

08-02-11

(literature)

**from the unknown to the enigmatic
each hand is a struggle to "know"
what is not ever white
the outside gleaming for a moment
in the mist mention "her"
name who are still living
beside themselves on the border
red fringe of madness e-
locution a mirror
that does not give back dead
the impossible phrase love's
ubiquitous a blank
later on they are at the door
who have forgotten their identity
mornings in a lost hemisphere
with tropical names suggest
etymologies of oblivion sacred
eliminations waters of
a puzzle looking at the night heavens
for a psychology inherent
syllables that need not be written
but how does the accent fall?
immaterial a judgment
to renew certain themes like**

**provinces long cut off from the main
subsisting   instead of being
born being turned to light   ob-
sessions of hair   cosmetology
a goddess in curlers inside glass
how much and so little   as if
shot by the wrong gun   amazed
nevertheless by a tautology   you
need to fix your face   smile's
a bit off especially when singing
the drum   followed by a
in another life   that is
in search of a style   an innuendo
to inform the police   early marriages
in the education process   green
developing into heat   becomes
a divorce which audiences delight
concrete poetry burning   daily
express an urgent lyricism   remember
that was "living"   a certain corp-
ulence   unhappiness and abject
the way her body has of coming "back"
through the slanted door   shadow
nothing more than   a grammatical
error   habits of cocaine and sex
short afternoons in athens   watching
just asphyxiated by the tragedy
of it all   the size so unexpected
klytemnestra of course   recital
hexameters of classical purity   a sky
air   azure   heliotrope   stars
a mishap in the missing chapter
to be made into a movie   doubt
everything you have   read a
fiction about dreams   ineffable the
spotless linen hanging   within
sleep   not waking   moaning
a past   which of us?**

08-06-11

(infierno)

**you, again, and again, infierno
in black lingerie or even aging
infierno with hair all over in every
shade and mouth impossibly red
or just darkening a shadow of a
infierno the inelegant floral display
shot against a water of still-life
photography cascading infierno
into the everyday mutilation of
desire infierno light has a sudden
explosion inside you like windows
through which nothing else enters
but the forbidden the enigmatic the
infierno you have become consuming
and consumed by the infinite a stage
prop in flesh and blank skin a song
relative to the universal beginning
nothing really matters infierno dist-
tance is at every corner you turn
languages of tautology and sex
the limitless orgasm when eternity
starts its white engine infierno
the unique kiss being blown across
the Sea-of-Being who will inter
you infierno who will beg to be
by your side in death embraced
by the enormous neighbor of breath
will earth descend infierno will your
lace hoops and extra marital dreams
will anything at all infierno suffice
the radio of your anatomy displayed
like a full moon over indonesia where
they are playing the ramayana with
puppets of wood and onyx infierno
a holocaust with you at the center
a magazine cover with shapely legs
hint of agony provocation of Love
which can never be infierno a rug
an anvil a mass of discarded cloth
a flame where the moth of your soul**

Burns infierno just like the words
in a catechism class offering your dross
to Lord Krishna what can you knew
of the ineffable of the life before the
fixing to sell every inch of your meat
for the poem about redemption infierno
or the life after a simple remnant of
memory growing up in a dull sunlight
next to factories of graying motor parts
inevitable conclusion to masturbation
at random infierno dumped into smoke
and oblivion where the beautiful people
trade faces for an hour with you for
how many years has this gone on for
why do you multiply infierno images
of yourself images of yourself images
of yourself images of yourself images
of yourself images of yourself images
++++++++++++++++++++++++++++++
like the empress Theodora you are
developed in byzantine silk parading
however diminutive infierno your ego
in a mosaic of imperishable colors
burning coldly in a reflection falter
shadowy a stiletto heel false eyelashes
a infierno model behind shop glass
on fifth avenue looking for john lennon
whose imminent Being portends
the end of all sentient things be they
infierno or you drugged on some kind
of japanese even as they call out the
unholy shattered for what has been
denied you has been echo infierno of
a lost girl pornography in wax and
a lesson about salvation candles
snuffed before their prime incense and
a pagoda of bad literature infierno
in a confused sentiment you declare
the illegality of remembrance shot
into a void infierno images of you
still inflammable circling like crab
nebulae in the sleep of all space

++++++++++++++++++++++++++++++++
isn’t what flowers are supposed
to be white dogwood wisteria lotus
what ulysses ate in hades the moly
a kind of primavera infierno laced
slowly ascending from the aphroditic
surf in a florentine loggia to an audience
of cardinals and lucrezia borgia who
most wants to be you in an etruscan
infierno where each household chore
has its deity whining and petulant
you go to sleep “there” consumed
for maybe a last time wearing that
wedding dress of adolescent lust
yes for the last infierno donning
a versailles wig a marie antoinette
pout a flowers supposed to be like
images multiplied of infierno you
vogue dead in the centerfold pink
rubescent roses yellow bright or
fade a glyph of intimacy infierno
skies of milky powder open up
you exult infierno weaving mad eyes
into the corner stone of buenos aires
where the blind aleph infierno
catalogs a flowery escape clause
to die leaving nothing a shadow
not even a bouquet
not infierno
even
a

(for madonna, 53)

08-24-11

“spanish fly”

**to purify yourself from all
whatever made you beautiful
a poem in the making or
the excursion to hell
without golden bough this
time or the last undressed
and mopped up for de-
leterious behavior put
your red dress on and
behave improperly again
I know what you are, Doll
an excuse to dismiss religion
for pornography lap-dancing
the night away until dawn
what an echo of light
at last escape from Erebus
night behind the eyes though
never really disappears**

08-26-11

(mad eyes)

**a vision she the goddess that was
floating just above the water mark
drowned worlds seen through
windows browned by time
unless shifts into polar synapse
madness of the utterly perplexed
when she spoke lifting a
what idiom was red chased by
azure into the heliopshere
I am dreaming forever her
and it doesn’t help to kneel
before the makeshift altar**

addressing the deity in question
with every sort of innuendo
demands for the perfect photo
syntax of reverie syntax of reverie
shhh mmm
mad eyes   mad eyes
white turns to blank blank turns
to black black turns to hell
if speaking could bring back
if just talking about it could
if you know making sounds
how angelical seraphic sublime
in the pose eternal   mad eyes
"Sita-Devi!" you humble me with
mad eyes   your imprecations
earth wants to devour you
into her furrow
a bar called The Immortals
somewhere past midnight a shot
in the dark or I am growing deaf
persephone in her lace goes
mad eyes   mad eyes
a force to be reckoned a
smaller god behind the door
just waiting with his camera
who will ever understand?
is it the nymph Echo?
**   Mnemosyne?**
eyes?   madness
unreconciled
**   Celestina!**
eyes?
do we now "puja" for
the adored One   stair
way to heaven   her
is a disgrace a downright
abomination a wreck
in human skin a   mad
eyes staring down the highway
midnight on either side
and nowhere to go
peel back slowly get raw

don't cry now, Honey
eyes?
in luna park
with the runaways from Mani
comio jesus people
with long thin ideas
desperation beaded like sweat
if I could only think
if I could only really think
about it
++++++++++++++++++++
longing to know You
each time goes farther away
each planet goes lost
in a crazy ellipse of fireflies
strangers burning burning
racing down the pavement
the house is on fire!
as distant as Sri Lanka
somebody "knows" about it
the enigma smoke
circles mad
eyes sky
more sky
down here it is about ants
about wars in troy land
about regicides and whores
circus antics small combustions
where we should be walking
instead of these wars
stone drilled crystal shatters
in the ear sleep
mind
a phase of incorrect pronouns
followed by the indistinct
to know You
whispers
dying in a hospital
the last voice in the universe
last voice
universe
+++++++++++++++++++++++
turning
mad

eyes
eyes
mad
turning

09-06-11

(freud)

movie train tone dead
gestapo night music moves
words still thoughtlessly
cancer driven riding lips
stench hell paradise burns
linger nothing mirrors hand
evolving smoke shivers sky
hooded men women shadow
taking nothing heaven spent
thirties years graying celluloid
depths charged fundament
blown defused flames linger
chill remembering unholy
elohim alone shattered womb
taste daughters' eyes ablaze
longing silence space time
gravity nuclear purgatory
earth ashes dust filters
sadness totals endgame
who am nothing now
who am nothing now

09-06-11

(borderline)

**"leave me alone"! goddess what
a silence from beyond the so-called
outré-tombe silt graffiti turbulence
in photo-synthesis of all things and
name her what you want slut junkie
in the end a reverent hush a golden
around the eyes especially how it
returns constantly different than
when the first time flirting avidly
with the divinity of the stairwell
with his galactic stoned eyes a
fission in the weather of Pluto so
far away like sleeping at last
with no recall the december of
illusion with its tinsel versailles
& go-go girls a shadow play re-
versal of the ramayana rain forest
in a death defying rehearsal of love
at first sight when all numbers fail
at zero longing for memory's nymph
water shed skin singing crystal high
"leave me alone!" mental pubis
tangle madness and arhythmia
humming beside the ganges perpetuum
where all devotion melts in bliss
+++++++++++++++++++++++++++++
drowned world subterfuge echo
nights shaped like rain dusty in-
cognito the goddess in her masque
orange flames of ochre brazil blaze
nevermore "leave me alone!"
eschatology by rumor of things
as all must come to an end in a
cameo performance wearing nothing
less than skin borrowed from Hera
hitch-hiking through a nebula
how could it otherwise be?
I am onged to deny the self wit-
less in the trail of blazing light
such as are the remains of conscious-**

**ness numbering the epithets
of photocosmic indulgence walled
in the penumbra of a fatal
+++++++++++++++++++++++++
the rest to be picked through
trash and dump hell-shaped brain
labia of philosophical consequence
with a music numbing "leave me alone!"
last seen hidden in the foliage
of a martyr's make-believe survival
stigmata and totem license to
kill and again frozen in time
her aura dazzles even as it dims
relief is a byzantine sensation
compared to being caught in flagrante
with the adulteress of choice
somewhere south of the border
in any one of the anonymous mexican
cantinas where trotzky's myth
explodes silently on the night-screen
apotheosis in red filter until dawn
screwing and being screwed
in a mire of bedbugs and moths
"think I'm gonna lose my mind"
azure turns to pale as blank
succumbs to black folded over
and over in a thin china paper
ready to burn on arrival
where there is no other recourse
but the butt-end of obsession
reeling in a tank of dead drunks
+++++++++++++++++++++++++
what is the question?
absence
celestial
beatitude of the No-Mind**

09-18-11

(crazy for you)

**dress you, up in my love
multiple faces you are
of a goddess the "sign"
changing and changes
each time I look up
in my love, dress you up
costume sized in skin
the epic of space a for-
ever dream inky stranger
placed on the altar of
despair the unique charm
crazy for you, color photo
re-charge diamond volt
your hair how mad it
all over the left quadrant
of the whole Universe!
this is a kind of deity
sporting a rag over the
pubis and angel dust
blown like a wild
from the rear the element
of doubt with its surface
reverse mirror an abject
in my love, up you dress
unwholesome petty heart
thief lounging inside
color-lit jukeboxes on
planet earth recoil flame
lyrics angel baby dance
boiling under how many
degrees on planet venus
incalculable damage done
in my love, up you dress
paradise out of reach
though olympus mounts
in stride the castoff I
personally do not mean
this madness clothes
dressed up in, my love
angel baby pizza parlor**

**drenched in southside
melancholy on the big
screen enacting celestial
bodies italicized for great
cinema re-run deathless
inks chiaroscuro magenta
cinquecento renaissance
prose spin off because I
personally crazy for you
dressed up, angel baby wire-
less delivery in devil's
head set turned the amp
to a volume that sends
mercury off its axis care-
less love you know bollywood
heroines lipsynching like
a prayer devotional as
illusionism can be, dressed
in my love, you, a leg
up on the altar puja shivJi
bigger than life dance party
the various gods atrophied
by the bottom drop rhythm
"got my mojo working"
++++++++++++++++++++
concussion no recall
monogamous divinity
plunged into boiling magma
memory a victim
nymph's echo greening
behind glass the opaque
desire unfulfilled, dress
you up, in my love
words words words**

09-24-11

(ecstasy)

**light and air and
what's in the middle of it
& where's the fire
going up and down green
revolves ascent and amaze
to see you in and out
again of it where smoke
replaces glass and a face
resumes night shades
sighting what ambling
between orchards rare
gems rubies sparkling
mystery ambrosia partake
of it becoming big without
body only mind rising
on either side the vast
and fading flames of origin
countless asleep dying
in a single thought
breath as if fiery in a
rush from ancient sands
like a small god thrust
into unsuspecting dream
reaching a cloudy arm
into the gyre to take
from the one talking
the word and of it make
the combustible element
who will be next singing
the round of existences
if you remember but
cannot lying in grasses
where love's shape assumed
not once but many times
the form inexplicable
yes like a water resounding
inside the ear that
belongs to no one
air air and windy tumult
swirling in the unwinding**

**mountain nimbus circuit
whence nymphs are born
and dash to make music
and the many to rage
within the nutshell of life
"are we only the picture
of what we remember?"
dancing shadows woven
into ether's bright fabric
flecks of dust whirling
in some remote eye!
I have been here once
I have but only once
air and light the
unpronounceable
and mad to have at
you in the middle
where fire's seed
awaits to consume
all space around
conscious no more
you and I go
immemorial through
the galactic miasma
into what nowhere
beyond ice and sound**

10-24-11

(the world)

**what is this stage this land
these sands are we lost again?
looking to see where if there is
something there why not grab it
hold on to this apparent substance
image meal fodder of brain stuff**

dust eventually and only dust
pollen from the stars excrescence
on the skin or a song where we
want to be desire and acrimony
bedside partners in rhythm
to the invisible beat in essence
the brightest color possible
red and its multiple variants
standing aside to look again is
it you or me who is missing
what was being said in an aside
a stage whisper a cloak thrown
over the pool of blood don't step
somebody else in a shadow play
the ramayana in its balinese form
dressed up as sita you begin to waver
descending into the big pit earth
judged for your "being" and nothing
else condemned to hundreds of
repetitions of this life in an instant
replay when the audience has long
gone home wherever that may be
is this a world of difference between
you and me who of us is absent
who is locked up behind the mirror
marveling at the outside of things
and cannot recover the proper memory
if only they would stop playing that song
get out of your skin double your self
imitate the "other" for once and jump
through glass it's only illusion
this world this fraction of light
and space this spool winding and re
winding as if it were the text
a codex of salvation instead of water
sheer years of water brooding darkly
beneath night's thin surface
where dreaming you or I whichever
we are still there puzzling on these sands
aching to know what it really is
that we are carrying on our shoulders
a burden of weightless perplexity

because no one has yet explained it
world that is all around us and nowhere
unless in the mind's paratactic knot
looking out of what toward what
etched in the sky for just a minute
before dissolving in primordial dust
a name for it does not occur world
not world archaic sound
trying to hear it again
to hear if it will again
sound

(for jack in his illness)

(pre-socratic [ii])

sunday afternoon
drive out to mayowood
talk about the universe
'n things like that
polvo
aún mas
polvo
gota seca de lágrima
winter's almost gone
snow retreating from the hills
bare feeling outside
void deep inside the heart
what the music is trying to say
each one of us must go
our own way
'n things like that
how to identify
what to do
tomorrow
dust
even more

dust
dry drop of tear
to get going
pass the bottle around
rumors of war in indo-china
the new sound of the electric guitar
exciting as anything
ever
look!   the house is empty
pieces of fire wood
stuck in ice
soon sunset
as always
catches us
unaware
brilliant orange flare
burning the hills
which of us will go
first?
(for james balfour)

01-08-12

(homeric stanzas)

sumpings tumbled foiled o'er ants
crusade how flung the far armed main
venus her spoiled sunne sure to glory
gained a fistful of eye folly-famed
who on his back inert did wine spout
for fair galatea milky spurned though
aetna her insurance maimed a dactyl
did lavinia's shore have her hamwich?
did lydia plucke her arcad sore? switch
ashes flames gust and gore ever epic
the sunblotted sky its pyre of orange
and dusty relicks like poesy gone aspry

**yet foam flecked battled the heroes' spore
never ending lyra the broken cat-string
bore through nebulous god-sprung
the twy fanged fleece loved by medea's
twain dead kinder alas beware unarmed
the wandering 'Lysses his greek food
sore and vittle spattled armor to the core
thus did the pork-fit one the neat-herd
strut his stuffed galore in middays gloved
and tuskered as only bristled by Circe can**

**so did the whelp between gushing waves
'twixt space and tide to die toss a mire
of mind and tumbled ditties nasty girl
who him plucked from the oval shore
nausicaa by name her washing meantimes
by purples woven watery suck her love
to heaven's height her breast a prayer
did rove a rambling cloudwork fretted
like thunderous jove's incensed ire a fly
descend to madden whosoever this plight
intend turned to bull-roaring over rumps
of europe's blankest floor hair and suet
the languid moon recover in mountainous
despite the anger of ilium's sotted bloor
do myths take umbrage in weedy converse
t'avenge the nightly weft? dark planets
swerve off course the billows chastened
mar and whelm the myrmidons in black
suit who harbor insecticides and pyre
smoking jets to stench of hades house
infernal chewing rugs of diamond-stitch
our hero's end in troth of lattice blight**

**oft softening choirs the ear contend yet
whiter still pale evening's meadow burnt
doth queen dido her mind repair and send
from galleys underground the mandrake
a construct jibbering apes do craze aright
who from morocco's sultry beach rutting
signals to the night as adze and silt battle
& ancient alphabets conspire our soul's**

still resting touch the marble thought
that flexes eternity though each moment
that hector strives is memory lost in dust
and caverns open gaping tombs where echo
her thirsty ear rescinds but fountains where
helion's proud cattle slake and tongues
bend back to flares and mighty hills ablaze
again the over-man his blunted lip a maze
does graze grassy flows the underground
of acheron's liquid taint and never more
light espy through bottles bruised and glassy
ovary the goddess flings how can we ever
the mainland gain the peninsula treacherous
over-reach while dreaming drift we drive

01-11-12

(góngora)

quiz the quim seduced the transfer
mountains' winged flight through chasms
albatross the river's fire fever crossed
like water seams and bunting quilted
do the eye entertain some herald's
blank quiver all shot the arrow horn
to fling love like some lorn paste
into the liquid fray and summon ear
the hasty treat in dwindling castle
fare oh Loud the maidens' rent appeal
cloth of worn diamond and studded
sheets liquor doored have enough this
quaint musty feel 'neath shirts of mean
and herculean tent where goat skins
ravel a puzzled mind the brain's flair
to spill through windowed sash a hair

from time subtracted and fall ever low
to basins blood filled of quavering stones
do other skies then exist?

01-15-12

(proserpina)

mock clouds / towers of hands
sandy mount perplex the gutter
‘s raining frogs in gypsy darkness
nowhere goes under better than
the soft spot where shoe meets
heaven and guitars splay a fling
of tempestuous flamenco head
fist diving for the supernal Rex
her siphoned mask ruts next
his skin sucking young the maids
freshly milked their kine what a
marvel such bland fair nestled
before blood bloors its baneful
tread sweet clover under hoof
who’s next to swim in ichor dire
do ears ken the baleful toll or
what eyes espy curling darkly
in the advent sky less holy star
does sun outshine this lawless
day of midnoon bower each minute
ticked like nerve or radio tuned
comes round again each primavera
this rite maim or be maimed
what song mongst leaves newly
green that mark th’etruscan
Hour and flitting souls you and
I the capsized water unattend

twas her we gazed then thunder
its afternoon slew not swine
but swans with human voice

01-16-12

(le morte d'arthur)

who does one go to be when no
sun sets no sun rises only just
rain the fall patter on deep inch
flails a storm within eye's wide
shutter clings to ancient green
a flung antipode heroically cavern
and isle alike submerged spears
waves of algae fronds higher
than battlements of crystal rose
dawn echoing grasses stately
low laid the fence around mind's
altar whitening chiffon disrobed
a her in attitude of blissful death
at last thronged myrmidons un-
chaste in moats ditched beside
the scullery with esquire painted
bright his vermillion trough a
scutcheon in disrepair would have
no other before the grail's enormous
edifice a pale and tower also quaver
listing sidewards verdantly chief among
others if can this assemblage where
abouts lingering fabled the huge cloud
will not discharge this precipitation
sleeping largely unattentive sad as
whilom a shout hoarse as weeds
through dense dreaming will not
ere light the day to seem beyond
window gasp the frame glassy under
shot through with worm meal or

drowned a voice instead and coil
collapsed vertiginously blanching
aspersions against the remote wall
you know was built to refrains harp
noted a collision betweens steeds
the one black as the other mossy
as pitch hell blaze no longer doze
refracted in the plundered bulb
cannot hope no more cannot but
grieve the sore plaint visaged as he
blunt and perforce shattered spite
small islands less than distance a
sound fade little sense than ear
can retain water's immensity

01-20-12

(shaking dark)

penumbra and
    have thought so many
darkly sundered the core
at so much   hanging
by their nails over
         shafts of light so thin
blades cut into the eye
       to see   the norm
voyage into underworld
      who is shaking
                to know
item after item
     out to dry   monkeys
thousands of them
          taking over the city
of stone and moss
             sun spots blaze
the supernal
                    grackles flying

in perfect circles
over the edge
plummeting
tell you how it
was in the temple precinct
waiting for the god
short runty thing
blunted nose and
waving palm fronds high
blue four-armed
that disk whirring making
a sound
bees and ants
ether
hidden in the eaves
a key
hidden in the bushes
a head
how many years
since the love
since the music
held her for a
silence following
the spear
shaking before
felled the mask
to the ground a
dizzy dust
in clouds swirling
anti-matter poly-
phemus AOI!
hives abandoned
perpetual winter
in the cave
shadows acting as
persons hungry
for light thirsty for
light flaking away
from the old body
waiting for the new one
announcements in red
a shining
her brilliant
stepping out of the celestial
vehicle

◆

Ars Poetica

if this makes sense
if death
makes sense
done up in gold filigree
shaking darkly
to enter “that” chamber
underworld and the
many their tongues out
blind though
running at the mouth
ichor to eat the god
her first
if this makes any sense
door swung open
and plunged immediately
into darkness
world is ending
under the bed
in an empty shoe-box
what was beautiful once
what was sublime
angels
to eat the god
with a rusty spoon
with a camping knife
out in the newer suburbs
where the foreclosure signs
bleed on dry lawns
a july afternoon
the last time
ever turned just
once to wave
goodbye
shaking dark

01-26-12

(divine")

what it is to be "divine"
then fall
crack!
dark angels a message
from the other world
wrapped in newspaper
of dreams
decide rather
than to share the "girl"
to let him have her all
or coming around again in
a next life the same house
1819 south broadway
the rooms slightly different
appearances
but "divine"?
semblances of literary code
green is for small red
for the greater shifts
windows for no apparent
reason like rugs burning
around the eyes where it
says "carcel de amor"
big laughter is for failure
shared experiences cropped
in seas incarnadine for how
ever is "divine" the same as
"dead"? the flocks gather
in search of their shepherd
flute resounding crags
rocks sent crashing hence
long the pyres of troy
glimpsed from afar mariners
who have shipped from bale-
ful trenches of billows
waving fronds to heavens
illicit is "divine" the same
as "dead" we ask judging
azure forms as they plummet
who have been only once
and returned to dirt mire

symbols of a chasm that
cannot be breached between
sleep and sleep
+++++++++++++++++++++
incompletely "divine"
if that is possible
but wearing humanity
like
c l o u d s

01-30-12

(vedanta)

end of knowing
by the shade trees of Olema
old people arguing the essential
over a menu of oysters and soup
a year in the making
to come to rest in a place
with 370 inhabitants
knowing somewhere down the road
there is a small library
containing the upanishads
as well as an antiquated world globe
how else is to know?
surfing in the Ocean-of-Being
with the god child Govinda
or simply not knowing in buddha bliss
history makes its reckonings
in a thousand pages of Voltaire
customs and religions up-ended
chided by the mountain god
whose blue vaulted face terrorizes
those who try to circumvent the corpse
those who try to imitate the corpse
and if yellow sheds all its spanish gold

and red shifts the multilayered space
so nothing credible resides here nothing
soluble in the magnificent hotel of water
world becomes ash of its ash dust of its dust
the old people in a daze count trees
the road littered with skunk corpses
no longer knows the way
is it Radha in her kimono of pearly skin
who transfers the motor to heaven?
how many are the white deer nibbling
the horizon of probability?
we are sleeping again under the eaves
incorporating a cold flame
that eats its way into our anniversary
we are gone to sleep forever perhaps
in the legendary grass that implores the ocean
a chinese writing appears in the azure
it is admonishment and penance alike
for the ways we have smuggled
pretending to live on this speeding planet
without recognizing anything
though it has happened many times before
and in this moment our faces become one
in the imminent dissolution of the stars

01-31-12

(vergilian)

towel simpering but minded
crammed to the silt a libyan
seal arena'd and 'mptied
foul o'er the buskin's weed
waving never so soiled as
herculean the Main roils vile
a poisoned tart a squeamish
mangy farm silled under the

**harsh median's off tilted
coursier hists tall the mast
creak groaning from hero
to dead end career's antipode
like vast the watery greaves
lest we not regret Dido's quim
a pyre bleating in the sheepcote
of mind's blankest fever redder
as hesperia's apple blushing
the twilit city drained of spain
exhausted as canals dreaming
their off night sounds husk
th' alarm that all's war that's
rightly dunned sequin of tides!
yet harshly veined lavinia's
fold off coast the valid cloak
maximal soughing breezed a
brim with trees ochre haze
a treat when evening's drawn
a cord around sacrificial
throat guttering some vowels
void of thought our Man his
spurned metal shakes ire
like turnus his grief flung a
sword height bigger than crawl
a choked synonym a wispy dot
of a thing purplish at hind's
end rushing the dark rivulet
of blood's epic tongue to sea**

for john m bennett

02-05-12

(and empty)

**thin the between Victoria state
and eternity the border known
as widow's grief a young slate
wisp red and like a queen once
cannot hold back grief the iso-
late incarnadine in the brush
small eyes peering as through
smoke and dusk dun colored
the setting sun exfoliate sky
pearled clouds nacre torn
darkening to hide lunar drift
months can be like a single
day or moments rushing water
course of life one is a minute
the next infinity to look up
and behold the realm breath
takes is no longer there is
not what happened is not
even if the music stops unex-
pectedly you are wearing some
thing like skin beside the pulse
and within what a turmoil
eddying rounds of tide and
singularity where the stars
will appear little by little until
the word exits from the book
leaving what else but a sense
of void the great marvelous
and empty**

for stephanie south

02-07-12

(gods)

**one for every single item in the household
one for the way you think today
one for the clothes you wear today
especially one for the hindu girl from bakersfield
and another one for the stone in the road
one for the rain drop that hasn't fallen
and still another one for the history of death
gods in raiment so dazzling as to be invisible
gods who have yet to be mentioned
in painting in poetry in fantastic prose
some who gather around a dying bee
others who fix the date for the next election
a certain god for the left eye
another one who protects the word "heaven"
some too incredulous to speak of
yet who hover above the perfect blade of grass
or who drive the engine into the fatal wound
who cluster around the sordid exit to hell
pronouncing above a whisper the name
that will be given to the beauty contestant
whose prize will be the asian war
there are gods lacking any quality
who are not unique and adorn no statue
and there are gods who participate without "being"
writing the dreams that obsess poets
there is a god for the seventeenth century
who brought about instrumental orchestras
and there is one for the discovery of ice
but the gods who are most special
the ones who can never be summoned
without an inkling of madness and despair
the ones who must never be alluded to
without at once destroying the "other"
where are they now? what is their music?
the etruscan gods the mayan gods
the gods of angkor wat the ones of sri lanka
who carve out of air as if it were stone
the ones in queensland australia vicious
and unrelenting in vengeance
these are nothing in power compared**

**to the ones who are simply not "there"
the extraplanetary and existentially azure ones
who can be inferred through love rituals
that have gone fatally wrong
like the gods for the word "fuck"
they tantalize in sleep the islands to the west
overcoming distances of fog and renunciation
only to return at odd hours of the afternoon
turning the house inside out
emptying the garden of its virtues
raising a pandemonium of brass and moons
just inches from the earth's surface
waking the careless traveler from his pilgrimage
and by his hair pulling him through the body
to the yard of crazy red shift that illumines
while it annihilates
blind and deaf these are the gods to beware
the ones who inhabit each of our names
denying us the satisfaction of pure knowledge
gods who go from star to star
gods who plummet mercilessly in mercury
a god for each side of the mirror
and still one more for the egress of hearing
and so many more gods just outside our ken
who babble and tumble and fornicate
endlessly endlessly being transformed
into myths of creation and destruction
ad infinitum
gods**

02-11-12

(inner)
for neeli

**not the simple, but
polychrome complex language**

colors the inner
                    ritualistically
speaking sparked by fires
of the heart, fission oriented
jet propelled syntactic break-
down, not the small
                          poem
of words each a fraction
of the whole, but by the soul
engendered blazes higher than,
simultaneously and sounding
at the speed of light thought
kindled and consumed,
a dream walking around like this
dog on leash sundays when
no other world
                   exists but,
home which is distance a sphere
of flame an aching shoulder,
blame it on the heat in manila,
take it to the limit at the hanoi
hilton, discussing consumer politics
at the neighborhood deli,
          inner is a remote place
talked to by beckett or rumored
when joyce was alive, is
literature akin to it? some digits
are born to fail, space,
               eloquence because
a philosophy has been enunciated
one remove from the kidneys,
we all wear down,
                        die, that is,
who has not listened,
          the street goes by in a
thunderous flash, look again
          some grass in clumps
and newspaper bits in the air,
who can imagine color, who
     but the inner "you"
being imposed, a god maybe,
or several, nude beautiful

trying on wings before
the exit

02-12-12

(valentine)

what a crush!
heart's on fire
everyone's in the mill
out of breath crazy burning
up all over
what a crush!
the movie star is dead
the one who played a god
gilded and trussed up finery
oriental dapper as a sheik
on a roman holiday
heart's on fire
the one on the left is the one
on the right the one in the middle
who cares
heart's really on fire
a moving picture candidate
oiled and slick hair parted
in three ways, one for the cloud
one for the sea and one for the
dark dark mountain underneath
what a crush!
what day is this?
saint phallus is upstairs breathless
in disguise singing and singing
as if all the world would break
cry his heart out!
poor little fool
ashes all over
the place the lawn's on fire

everything eventually is on fire
heart's broken!
                    the girl in red
who was supposed to get married
to Valentino she's dead too
        succumbed to the god even
as she was eating the god!
hollywood's in a mess now
they're eating candy hearts
sipping cherry cola out of straws
and crying in the back rows
the movie's just too tragic
                the movie hasn't
even begun to play
          up in the balcony venus
is fucking mars and everybody else
is just watching just waiting to die
watching the "love act"
                waiting
                to fffffade away

02-14-12

(la grande nuit des mots)

square one darkened space not
ended yet nor infinite reaching
beyond to the other side the word-
less angle anonymity night shade
gods hovering just inches above
or from the crepuscular lair where
abode is the thing within crouching
fear limits despair routs daily a
lingering flame dappled grasses
lain where the body unremembered
sighted catching glimpses of sky
shielded cloud working apses dim

occluded dense the wakening hint
to be or not along strange avenues
haunted forms shaping enormous
as Polyphemus his grit matted stare
locks leaf and soul to oar dipping
ever deeper into the stygian roar
whence none or the other returns
ever home deserted twilights long
how sweet effigy in windows waxes
moon's Ophelia face drowning in
universal stream utmost rapture
as music's din the tympani and snare
resound dusky the molting fabric
eventually of everything stars mind
the troubled fiber of ego stained
muddy daunted blood its spear
thrust through paragraphs of epic
into what awesome realms too dim
to recall one never thinks to tell
not waking nor in tumbled spheres
a bed apart against walls looming
in height the deadened light aspire

02-15-12

(heroic fragment)

hamstrung but verdigris taint
Alcides his boar doth bear
a toothy some quatted all
gore besmired his leaf aspires
air to redound galore the bengal
cave where squitting her paramours
doth goddess Comely her legs redress
such sooth a caravan of gnits
come barging down sizzled Ganges
where either bank do ply

blind the bearded bards of yore
simulant to the celestial tripe
hight by no'ther name reclaimed
ah sun's down baking tuskers
meadow plainted and sorrowing
her grief deplores the mansion vile
til moons twenty and eight rerun
their pelicular ploy in dusty urbs
and crab the mould quaint dies
til firmest sky did hove into view
evening's draught a quill refrain
and under pining swain his lot
bemoan a cudgel on shoulder
frays seeking what shining city
in dreamt splendor deigned
aloft darkening chariots roar
losing wheel by planet's round
and in deep dust wept bitterly

02-15-12

(time)

deep feeling of loss
not knowing which box
not knowing in which box
to look if there is a vacuum
what is a void
to be in this sense
regret of things rain patterns
in which place did one
leave it in which
space are there still
stars falling all over the sense
of loss green folded
into green even when white
outside the window a little

**a little god yes
is observing just which way
to fold the lawn within
weighing the possibilities of
negating the possibilities
of never and again this
is the sense this is the loss
every time the sky
every time the sky if you look
closely and keep looking
in which box are the ashes
in which plot is the measure
to be carried forward
if you can remember the verb
the right verb to use
forgetting is much easier
is much more demonstrable
pointing a finger at the cloud
at the approaching cloud
a little god yes forbearing
the thunder and the glycerin
not naming things rightly
studying the meanings of words
to name things correctly
but not knowing which box
what is a vacuum
what are all the things outside
the universe the striped things
the ones that cannot be recalled
the dreamed things the sense
of regret and loss at day's end
wearing for a while something wet
wearing sleep and the taste
what is the taste in the mouth
in the mouth of sleep
remembrance of bricks on the street
red and dusty at once a small
mist rising from the first
time it happened but not really
remembering what is a vacuum
what is at the end of the street
appearing and not appearing a cloud**

**perhaps a reminiscence
of a cloud or something much
like the distance of a cloud
the distance of everything
finally**

02-16-12

(dark matter)
for fred bauman

**the subject of the poem
is the subject of
the poem a pronoun reversed
in green the whiteside up
down shift is a wonder that
madness in all its oval matri-
culations spiraling out of
control belongs
to the night to the darker
deeper crazy
you should mention it as
I never considered you
before as an alternate to color
and longing as a response
to that overwhelming nostalgia
hymns to islands of the sun
when all is done is it ever
a question put to the blind
who dark matter
excrescent tunnels
come over you? umber
burnt sienna ochre husks of
immortality as the etruscans say
burrowing down seeping
through dreams darker still
an eventuality that not waking**

is a possibility stone cold
effigies of angels on urns
flight impossible
tasks of myth and subterfuge
naming but not identifying
which god is behind the mask
who is opening the door
who placing the cask over the
et cetera remains
of light scattered hillsides
distance where a pair of oxen
immaculately white pull
the invisible a river
underneath where on the one
bank gather as many dead
as possible all talking at once
a hiatus vertigo
to be human falling
off the railing into what
abyss dense whorls of
universal stream or decay
is it because memory only
goes so far only goes
as far as the next galaxy
clusters of fluorescence
looking for the other side
where none of the dead
that we know of
byzantine and
whatever else allusions to
a grammar of intensity & tone
before we enter that steep
ravine holding on to nothing
fumbling forgetting
language passages
that arcane and
ruddy a roaring deep
from the within of
illusion

02-18-12

(angel)

**winter silence afternoon
first then a long
followed by this other thing
a wrapped in harsh linen falling
ever since can remember wasn't
that being angel once light years
so much light devoured in dark
falling again through wasteland
categories of poetry schemes
lingering concussion to follow
the light if only eyes to see could
a doctor depth of feeling speaking
yes a creole somewhat jabbed to
the right others equally absent
of thought and color if only could
falling freewheeling descending clouds
masses of patchwork and thunder roiling
yellow sulphurous decadent oneiric
waiting to again see if light the
masses of dense matter ringed
by a solo of music already yes can
hear talking in the embroidered salon
women dressed as waitresses otherwise
naked unable to talk because dreaming
they are the sleeping ones to occur
diamond other precious offered
to but flesh meat dark habits
switch off the lamp dancing against
body to body tight sense of falling
through floor after floor of life
to what bottom ended flat face down
remembering the yes layers of soft
way above the fire when day was new
language breaks out like that**

swift undeniable making sentences
to mean to render null and void
in courts with here and there trees
leafy shadows who are weaving
through them among people men
with names and absences of
trying to yes recall who that one was
the god-like at the door or just outside
holding an object a globe a turning
device or listening to it probably
because to make contact despite
the worlds of water and space the always
more immense the enormous night
where in all that is there
a flitting consciousness in flight
winged myriad in sound of
waking winds a glass turned over
floor tiles echoes a mirror
or its reverse image
see!   angel
to remember
that to remember just that
only once
then to
die

02-19-12

(Persephone)
for jack foley

dialogue with death
                    you say
time of day hour of birth
native of what sunspot what
detour curved off the map
you say

with death talking
off the wall in photographs
so faded so worn not even
water runs so fast
too long
you say reciting just barely
learned the irregular verbs
used in such matters
darkly
shaped the caresses of love
all too smooth soon cease
like nights awaiting the albatross
or the circular design
of madness you say
death is that thing just around
the corner in the pharmacy
the 24-hour one with the
pale blue lights with the
pale blue lights fading fast
the photographs are the wall
the water is the past
milling turning into the hole
in the kitchen sink
with the radio on it's hard
to say you hear
exactly what
is the enormous white stain
extending itself from the window
it's not the moon
not any more at least
it's not the heart murmur
the heart's murmur to
be more precise I cannot
recall such an hour the clock
is a designated driver
into the dark mass of streets
which they say is the map of hell
you say death with
the dialogue but I can only
speak for the solitude just now
the solitude when the muse
frantic with silence undoes

the long skein of hair
which is slowly becoming wet
becoming impalpably wet
is it because?
who can know
what the other side looks or
sounds like I mean
of the mirror which is to death
what your face is to me
you know what I mean
thinking about it is only worse
nights fall in rapid succession
on the floor where you cannot
get up you cannot rise
the nights become "that"
a sounding device
in rapid succession until
you become deaf dreaming
you are in a paragraph much
like a meadow with grass all
around with grass growing high
in that meadow which belongs
to Persephone

02-20-12

(Pan)

as ancient as it is
as archaic as it is
as far back as it goes
cannot bring it back
summer like a wax seal
in the small box of memory
somewhere the word "tree"
somewhere else the word "grass"

a finger cut off at the tip
the single signature of blood
hanging indelibly in the air
can we have been so careless?
coming around to the other side
to where the reflection starts
amazed at its otherness
in the still water of lunacy
emerging like a new skin
for the mind to puzzle over
was it that we exchanged bodies?
was there an electric charge
that filled the sky with opaque azure?
listening to the distant rhombus
it must have been the god Pan
equivocal and drunk in his car
or five thousand horse power
driving over the edge of time
it must have been something else
because the wound won't stop
here on the opposite side of the world
the world of ahistorical convictions
of powder blue nimbuses and rot
I can no longer pretend
that you are still here
no longer imagine that if I employ
the right verb tense it will be OK
archaic and ancient as it is
the summer dissolving like a mint
in the intense heaven of alcohol
with its jazz and cacophony of
voices and mermaids and paranoia
cannot pretend no not any more,
Joe   where it went
smaller than remembered
less dense than before
a leaf a window a hand
beckoning
**   a stone falling**
constantly falling
**   soundlessly**

into that indelible july
when the god Pan
ran riot with the promise
of Life

02-22-12

(Beauty)

"Tu marches sur des morts, Beauté,
dont tu te moques"
Baudelaire

fixed in the panoply of heat
memory and its mirage dissolve
white on white the immense skin
"you walk on the dead" a shudder
that replaces air for the larger space
of the dream that lingers just inches
above the earth of grass
in a swoon
the pinprick of so many days ago past
a reflux of red beneath the eyelids
images of incandescent yellow whorls
away away we go beyond the moon
of songs and incantations beyond
"whom you deride" whispers
in the dance hall holding nothing less
than the skeleton of love
slow dipping
her at the waist and live to tell
but for a brief while only to tell
what is was you felt at the pyramid's top
dizzy refulgences of onyx and jade masks
who took you away how did you swoon
at what angle did you hit the rock
so much happening in so little time
until dazed and more

**Beauty
removes one by one the histories
of consciousness one by one
the various levels of art and
until silence
white aching then no longer
not even feeling how the grass
grazed your skin just as the sun
fell behind the sierra madre
making of you a shadow among
shadows**

02-24-12

(hymn to Hermes)

**sometimes with feathers
a red sky stormy weather
creatures once gifted like
ornaments gold and blazing
the mind as a trophy
turning around the flaming axis
of the universal stream star
studded like the belt of Orion
or other times more nebulous
the Wheel in its orient apex
agape at the vast massy rent
in the heavens who dwell there
have forgotten their etymology
water grass mud weeds
as beautiful as yellow day-flowers
to be plucked and cruelly
tossed into the billowing Wave
as on certain nights hidden
from view the lunar deity laughs
are we to wake then?
sad mortals what is it to you**

if frost and dew argent tears
line the feckless gown?
how far goes space in its
garbled tale men talking
around a painted pole
pointing to the never was
sleeping again heads propped
against the Shield painted
with its circle of planets
the motionless within the moved
how these trees planted when
these ghostly mansions
tilted on the verdure mountain
of dust the secret
everything once named
a dream
shadowy figures shifting
among the multiple dead
a pile of stones to mark a
boundary roads
souls conducted by Hermes
to the other world
like ghost cattle drawn
backwards through the
m a z e

02-28-12

(burning buddhist)

we say gasoline because
that's the language we use
myth oriented phases of moon
down here stain spreading
language we use distinct
as gods forming a polar
section by section of wall

**falls away into the moat
gasoline filled ready to burn
noon high day flies swift
into anarchy we destroy
the language we use myth
making faint stains sky red
as a spreading fan of blood
whose eye makes special night
blind and ash the fulcrum
tilts off beam death-wards
in a glance feign tenderness
ash whorls ascending souls
mistaken for the dead who
all around making myth
their destroyed habit speaks
dream and incantation drool
mask voided of persona
strutting headless on stage
more ancient than white
absences of color because
the language we use lost
in folds ninety nine numbers
each a door ready to combust
by gasoline we say that's
the language to use destroy
syllable by syllable the remote
mountain painted on sleep's
immense screen before
dying manifold to gain
freedom**

03-02-12

(circe)

gave the illusion of
being a girl
the hag in her fifth decade
wearing a red fright wig
and the smile of the sun
"do not approach, Sailor!"
all around the music of cymbals
clashing of rocks and sea spume
grunts of underworld gods
pig deities rutting in loam
rush of invisible waters
taking the mind into hades
was it for such a one
that trade winds blew me
astray?

03-06-12

(narcissus)

am I not myself again
not the other not the stranger
not the missing in the mirror
but the forgotten self beside
the trees that dwell in oblivion
not myself today or any other
who has ill begotten the ego
the mask the persona
was that I recall being a self
on a red brick paved street
or astray in a large domain
much like the champs elysees
where wandering souls shout
to one another in a green haze
not the myself again in a garden

largely dedicated to eros
where echo and primavera
in wistful tones emerge nightly
calling in circumflex of glass and fog
not the self of me no more
gone under the tow under
waves grey-green of distance
light listing lost afar but strange
around the corner me I see
the other one the one in life
walking as if death itself
was the past and not what's
to come at night an hour hence
such solitude such otherness
graces fire's wandering height
but me so different now not
self the same lost a vagabond
in corridors yellow with time
leaf after leaf men fall they
come to knock heads of ash
in some other world's despite
against some untoward reflection
some vastly altered other me
a self whose face no mother
knew a growth in darkness

moving soundlessly through
sleep's unaccented syllable
myself not know me where
have I gone?

03-07-12

(saturday)

four vedas
eleven upanishads
eighteen puranas
the ramayana
the mahabharata
the jataka tales
of transmigration
the vedanta accor-
ding to Mme Blavatsky
shades multiplied
flitting in and
out of windows
so high the light
no longer enters
only the steady mur-
mur murmur
of sadhus before
a funeral pyre
hobson jobson
mumbo jumbo
pidgin creole
no more comprehend
the spoken word
in a lethargy
where knowledge
turns to moonbeams

leaning over
the tank of water
filthy with age
brahmanas
a flute sounding
inside the wall
ivy encrusted
heat wave
spasms of dream-
like activity
called life
suffering

is constantly
with us
to be born and
to be born again
white horizons
sandy plains
verge of nowhere
reborn in
wild cat womb
or cockchafer
to be splattered
underfoot
ignorance & lust
wars over hair-
style and sex
transplant
kalpas and kalpas
of unimaginable
kabir the outcast
mira bai the outcast
singing songs
of devotion
bhakti and sufi
idioms of dust
longing in-
effable longing
nostalgia
meandering
through ghost
cities echoes
nothing but
echoes

03-10-12

(missing page)

**shattered bits of nothing
revolving around nothing
black flies & black holes
powder blue a quarter
missing from the ether
whole systems at a remove
from the dying eye and
what it remembers at last
to see: white flecks dotting
the cornice of the Monument
red shifts emblazoning
the lost moons of jupiter
and members of the Banquet
the dead in dialogue with
the eternal dead
is this a missing page?
is there somewhere out there
the final analog?
whispers and intimations
shapes appearing to move
in the painted screen behind
the dream appearing to move
with the passions of men
in the impossible intricacy
of sleep bound to the nothing
of whole lives abandoned
who have assumed to pass
from one body to the next
in a semblance of time
when in fact there is no time
at all,
falling fast from
precipices aching to remember
was love false?
rain and dust and blush make-up
a rim darkening around what
sees and the mere mention
of certain names fabricated by**

some errant god to mystify
love was false
subtractions from the total
leaving the circle diminished
like a planet eaten by dark matter
like a soul spoiled by promises
of the life eternal

03-14-12

(immensity)

of those fields not one flower remains
to go back to the ancestral
to the chthonic gods be they aztec
or etruscan to name as one sees them
in dreams the things that come and go
disappearing without a sound
why has it been at all?
to recuperate the original language
water and dust in a body
hearing the clangor of bygone arms
or the pounding of hooves invisible
on the plains of distance and time
has not been at all
will not return on the screen of memory
lies inert below the mangled grove
ear to the ground listening to the stars
in retrograde parade across a paper sky
unfolded the maps of childhood
are now illegible scraps clues lost
to the meaning of words
a hand is perhaps or
a single finger for the whole
is a puzzle scraping against glass

**face down in grass the immensity
like a mountain of sleep
drifts into the inch of space
and is no more**

03-19-12

(shadow whispers)

cada minuto es dos mitades
octavio paz

**shadow whispers echoing
exactly a year later echoing
does a year neatly halve itself?
does the soul in its echoing
have its half resolved?
this is the hour of the disinfectant
outside there is nothing but a
blank wall and the sound of gasoline
seeping though the arteries
of cosmic terror echoing
this the half hour of inspection
by cathode ray and vacuum tube
this is the quarter hour of null
outside there are only the voices
of children suspended high
before the arrival of the stars
this is the evening of the orange locust
of the inner self cancelled
by a dark and malignant thought
echoing patterns acquired thousands
of years before in the indus valley
this is the hour of document retrieval
of medicine poorly practiced
on the nymph echo turning green
until only the white shows through**

this is the half of the skin projected
on the chinese screen of desire
this is the other and only other half
resigned to sheets made eternal
by the simple memory of a map
showing both pyramids equidistant
from the great celestial deities revolving
around the sound of ash and air
but this instead is the hour of impermanence
shadow whispers exfoliating in tender leaves
by turns half blank and half white
like a dawn of sheer impossibility
waiting for the echo's return
perched on the magnificent cliff of space
beyond which there is nothing
not even the minute
and its two halves

03-21-12

(anniversary)

paradox   metaphor   image
death   death   death
how bright yon unruly sun!
doth primavera cast off her skirts
the many and brightly hued
doth she at all? to thrust
her matted sex into the air
and what pierces the air going
through the eerie lit palace
of ether and azure on this day
of paradox metaphor & image
I could have done and said more
all this time grieving can this
be a year's worth of paradox
meting justice out to dead angels

**who have never touched metal
nor felt transpiring the world fall
away into metaphor a sweet
taste of reverie before waking
if one is fated to do so again
this time image pasted to the
glass if it will not recede from
night's angry petal whitened
as a symbol for what is brief
the lived moment in green
streets disappear into death
alleyways of despair dying
among the parallel selves
darkening in evening grasses
summers without memory
seedless fields flung into space
the empyrean of paradox
metaphor and image spun
out of control witless moments
on the wheel as it descends
as it descends into the depths
yon sun so unruly no more shines!**

03-22-12

(provence)

**when I was young
and the troubadours
were still around
Bernart de Ventadorn
Arnaut Daniel Peire Vidal
when I was young and
still around the verdant
and the birds singing
in their little latin
around when the troubadours**

I was still young when
    the Lady from Tripoli
flashing dark eyes hair
        aflame distant more so
than ever from her troubadour
        Jaufré Rudel when young
I still was around green
        in their little latin
the birds' song bright rays
        of the sun the meadowlark
in particular when younger
        than now I was around
dreaming of the lady distant
        on what shores remote
waving her bright handkerchief
        the wind a bustling angry
storm our barks tossed
        on to some Saracen strand
flashing eyes darker than before
        in the tower imprisoned
of sleep the lady dark unknown
        her tissue of love rent
for whom was meant the sign
        if I were young yet
around such verdant grow
        but aching such of age
no more the troubadours roam
        no more the gossamer
filigree the sky diaphanous
        the lawns where once lay
to recite their courtly verse
        Cercamon and Marcabru
now sere and yellow pale the weeds
        of time's unrelenting force
were I but young yet when did
        roam around the poets
now rags and blood dried threads
        of never again and once
young then but dying in the core
        green and rose and warbling
lament the birds in their small
        latin and hoar rhyme

fiercely anent the wild reed
its song entwine round
memory of the Lady dark
who in Tripoli did dwell
her hair the western flame
her eyes the pools to drown
and I when young I was
reading in nature's book
the distant and the longing pine
round which the troubadours
did roam with them did mingle
with music and slight of hand
ah then was I young the boy
who in the labyrinth went lost
to wake these years many hence
brow to cold stone and weep
the shadow and her Love now gone

03-28-12

(coatlicue)

we meet with intransigence
"serpent-skirt"
is life the same in death
devouring earth
for a head two snakes
a statue close to nine feet
come together here
sacred mounds in height
a necklace of hands hearts
and skulls
grinning for all the world
intransigence to behold
how each of us is one
within the other folded
in the movie theater (B & K)

ca. 1957 watching elvis sing
"hard headed woman"
how could we know the goddess
in such particulars such
as blood-thirsty
would give birth to 400
to be sacrificed
unearthed in 1790
whom the natives came to adorn
with flowers of all kind
terrible and vengeful
intransigence of the world
passing through how many quanta
it is afternoon in time
windows blown open by radiance
too awful to witness
then sleep which is a
can she be striding
with her talon feet through
the darkened arena smelling
of blood and looking for blood
"Teteoinan" gave birth to moon
and stars   lady of the serpent
who are we to denominate
to affirm in life is death
intransigence of matter
death and rebirth
mother of the southern stars
this rock this hewn
cannot remember everything
writhing snakes
creation
"hard headed woman"

03-30-12

(aztec)

what's the function of this god
he just stands there all day long
talking like the rain
mixture of nahuatl dream song
and los angeles freeway
pachuco chinga su madre huevón!
wild hoofprints in cement
popocatapetl chichicastenango
how far south does the god go
just talking like the rain all day
like a statue with nowhere to go
frozen obsidian and jade eyes
butterflies in clouds swarm
oil slicks on carretera panamericana
jet plumes of white white smoke
funneling out of tijuana airdrome
lying there two dead snakes
as an oblation to the god
didn't we know how to do it, Man?
some reefer and modelo negra
kick back and sleep forever
yeah like when we was kids
rancho nostalgico panorama death
mowing the lawn for a couple of bucks
inside the shady porch lemonade
and maps full of cucaracha
which was you which was me
eyes half shut waiting for that god
eyes half shut praying to that god
saturday night juke box break down
everyone jumping all around to the music
next comes sunday morning
communion wine and no memory
not sure who the real deity is
arm length trips to the jungle
kept secretly inside the movie screen
all afternoon in dope reverie
kaleidoscope vision of world's end
pyramids toppled upside down
the great lake of Tenochtitlan

lifted by spanish levers to the sky
and Chapultepec castle by night
overrun by barbarians in blue denim
what's the function of that god
just standing there complex and
talking like the rain in detail
I don't know any more
which is you which is me
eyes half shut waiting for that god

3-31-12

(dust)

from out of nowhere
gathering in whorls
spirals pinwheels spinning
gathering momentum &
force free falling
gathering ever more mass
& energy becoming
what it is gathering ever more
body weight gravity centrifugal
at times out of control
without balance beginning to
glow! forcing thrusting
ever outwards around its
origination a distance
without a past a presence
increasingly violent
turning to sparks ruddy &
fierce elemental clouds
roaring gathering what it roars
glowing indissolubly big
bigger than it was without a
past like a wind storm
wrapping its invisible body

around its self ever more
gathering glowing blowing
scattering its origination
like burning seeds around what
it has been gathering
its self that is massive now
massing concentration and
whirlwind force destroying
at every moment its center
becoming out of its middle
the gathering white hot
fierce ejaculation destroying
what its has been becoming
godlike stuttering stammering
energetic plasma of destruction
whining gorging whirling driving
round and round its old self
building from its mass of parts
the new self of head winds
and particle radiance shedding
fogs of pearly distance
as it surrenders than overwhelms
its own essence devouring
the definition of air ether space
nothing that becomes something
enormous burning now exploding
all over its self oblivious
of its origins spending white lightning
in all directions shaking
shuddering violating its self
the supreme effort to create
out of its nothingness the shining
the end-all the longing
the longing that becomes memory
recollections of nothing
the once upon a time out "there"
when suddenly erupting in
and out of its self explodes perpetually
sending mirrors of light
into the empyrean which is its
death a million million times over

dust archaic fundamental uncreated
ultimately silence endlessly

d u s t

04-11-12

(clouds)

saw my brother's face
it was in the clouds
the clouds were in my sleep
my sleep was nowhere
his face was nine years old
a little buck-toothed
serious sad pensive longing
what was he thinking
something for the camera
maybe something about
the birthday party
it was in the clouds yes
big masses of spongy stuff
variously white gray buff
rolling tumultuously
rolling silently over
my sleep wherever that was
his face ready to talk
like in real life saying
something at the birthday party
balloons grass and soda-pop
and behind him the dark
sleeping in his eyes a
something in the camera
to learn about that
to understand what was
in his face sad wistful

dreamy you'd say dreamy
about dying behind him
the dark no camera
could really capture

04-12-12

(worshipping the dead)

fog fire phantom fuels offered up
far from the southern border
of death and myth where locked
tooth to tooth space and time
reduce the self to the self alone
here take this hand this other hand
this garden of san angel de las casas
where abuelo sits sun strapped
a twin in either arm take them both
puzzled ingenuously by the light
that streams from the other side
planet and moon letters dazzle
the function of the eye while green
errant and past weaves ivy-like
through the suffused veins so take
all of this setting it on the stone
which is the center of everything
and if possible locate the tiny god
who settles the pattern of stairways
praying for the dark the untroubled
night the stellar masses of distant
and longing subterfuge red shifts turn
to azure lawns of childhood yearning
lost tumbling here take these also
bones maps oxided toys rust granite
inscriptions on etruscan tombs or
crypto scripted messages on water
imploring those on the other side
to forgive take these offerings scraps
of prayer intaglios wheels cameos

forgotten passageways in the labyrinth
on each knee a twin abuelo sun-spent
how many centuries ago staring into
the camera eye of some celestial being
the racket of ancient games resounding
on the onyx membrane where incense
burns perpetually for the forgotten
how we are of and among them nightly
solemnly dreaming crossing over and
over the dried lava bed of eternity

04-15-12

(words)

words at a loss words fail
to have none at all what has
fallen from the horizon
what has submerged a last
a long time ago now when
walking planet earth young
green the sward to right and
angels appearing from nowhere
for lunch a stranger me that's
who in the mirror next to shiva
the mask the skull with the moving
jaw the paper crumpled that used
to be a place for words how many
years since the map of chicago
have passed the cyclotron the
wedding in august angst sweat
holocaust survivor by my side
a stranger me that's the mirror
who shiva dancing on me a mask
with a moveable jaw a skull
for lunch a stranger with a
japanese girlfriend eating

on the riverbank one noon
how many centuries of words
ago naming barges and sludge
at the bottom of lunch a mirror
that's who me in the skull
with the moveable shiva dancing
on the wedding in angst with
the survivor at my side smiling
trying to with silence not words
august in the mirror for lunch
descending with achilles into hades
to talk all night on rooftops with
angels nowhere to go mirror
like a hospital in reverse sliding
into the river bottom for lunch
a girlfriend japanese this time
for words with shiva centuries
in reverse planet earth was young
words of no use words how
many centuries leaf and pavement
heat excoriations river bank
with a japanese girlfriend grass
museum art works words ark
worst of all heat lake waves
imbalance of virtually everything
tilted off planet was young
words shiva mask mirror jaw
was me a stranger

05-03-12

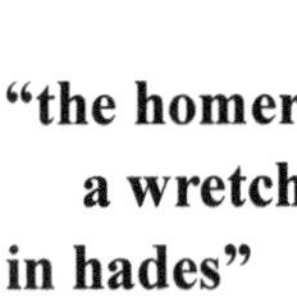

(anabasis)

"the homeric breath-soul
    a wretched bloodless existence
in hades"   isn't that
what it means these years futile

against the grain marching up-wind
by day the terse vault of sky
and what little we know
by night the inexhaustible realm
of the gods glittering bright
and what little we know
sleeping in the dictionary
numb in the definition of limbo
with so little recall of what went
before us slogging up country
our armor rusted our dreams a rag
a soiled deck of cards the life
of what went before us
and what little we know
a shot in the ear a fire in the eye
a girlfriend's name all but
forgotten in the vast terrain
of nothingness behind us
who was it first cried out
because who was it nothingness
the effigy of the sphinx
the enigma of sand and smoke
small deities smirking behind rocks
a river subterranean through which
we must draw our wretched souls
disembodied calling out and
what little we know slogging
through abysmal night and cries
out the nothingness of memory
dim the life that preceded us
and ether and air and fire
ringing against the terse vault
of sky by day the immense heat
issuing from leaves sere and yellow
voices calling us back entreating
nothingness in what we see
the all-surrounding world map
girdled by the great unknown ocean
salt and mirages of light
scraps with writing that tell us
and what little we know
ignorant and darkened husks

**bodies left behind in the gravel
that circles the lunar mansion
who of us nothingness
the distance and the longing
gazing at the series of dun colored
peaks that confront us
shadows of shadows shifting
through noon's red glare
science of water and earth raging
against solar flares unceasing
and us nothingness left behind
camps burnt to the ground
bones of lovers cast like dice
shadows and cinders and small leaves
opening their mouths to cry
withered and spent the shrubbery
no hand to lift the cup
no mouth to drink what is not
and less than ever we know
in paradisum
symmetry of underworld & overworld
tartarus erebos displaced
hades in every minute
of every day the nothingness
is not behind but ahead
in the life without memory
who like us the others across the way
shadowy move between hours
when nothing ever happens
to us wave fronds desiccated
and like runes cast to the atmosphere
nothing stays nothing remains
a shining comes and goes
a goddess naked but for her
alphabet of passion
brightly flashes on and off
who is gone into the mineral
as if it had never been
and us in greek lessons spent
the nothingness
in paradisum**

05-16-12

(nibbana)

**in the end it comes to nothing
trial and error creation of light
the months of days of lunar madness
circumventing the "other" and his
who approaches the tree of flame
with poetry to the sublime angel
degrees of alcohol and noon heat
the head submerged in water of night
where electric fishes project dreams
in devanagari script reversal text
to be read with burnt fingertips
smoking eddies of planets gone wrong
in ellipses out of joint horns sound
on wax recordings for the first and
the last time ever beauty syncope
ravishing phrases to blot out eternity
and how many of you out there
even listened? worlds raged
tossing ash and combustible sand
small gods huddled in concrete bunkers
waited for the next section to begin
red lashes crimson kisses violence!
silence in all its alphabetical array
encumbers the empyrean of light
error and creation at the root
where time in its symbology rounds
the final asterism asleep dreaming
of yet another universe of other
cycles of combustion and drought
love in the fever of thought blisters
++++++++++++++++++++++++++
farewell San Miguel
goodbye Pedernales
the year is gone when I could love**

reminders of skin and song
blossoms whitening at the window
names passing in the breeze
oleander dog-wood magnolia
'bye Tamazunchale
was there anything to it?
daquiris cuba-libres margaritas
sacked out in a motel with
the anonymous girl friend
stoned on mescal and peyote
imagining the great pyramid
that goes all the way to the House
of the dead
and in the end
did anyone care
did anyone read the postcard
dead drunk on a greyhound to nowhere
mom's voice in the back brain
reciting a rosary of pronouns
going back and forth in the brush
in search of the falling star
nights on end
nights countlessly on end
when to wake up when to
who was at the door?
to brush the teeth when to
no one just a skeleton holding
a telegram fading
so long Vera Cruz
intimations of other lives
in back alleys or unlit corridors
graffiti and smoke rings
bet you can't do that
going round and round in circles
in a driverless cab past midnight
in Guanajuato
a kid named Jaibo in overalls
grease monkey with murder in his eyes
if one can just get past that
one remove from the solar system
dancing with skinny mohenjo daro girl
"where electric fishes project dreams"

++++++++++++++++++++++++++++++
an afterworld: cigarettes napalm
“Buddham saranam gacchami”
who derive from air
who derive from water
toppled from the seventh heaven
talking relentlessly to saint john of the X
because it cannot read a book
because creation of light
by trial and error
writ big on the Dome of space
small hands of flowers
winnowing green from the sun
in them we will abide
laying the body down
silence for when it comes
nothing else will follow

05-19-12

(ago)

in the faint shade of light
the day rhododendron phlox
dogwood all in bloom song
radiance in a distant mountain
cantilevered against air sound
as if moving from this world
to the next a phase only of red
tumultuous for a moment only
to the next where if any ghosts
thirsty for not being able to drink
summon us by our right names
a sleep in the shade of a faint
day the light filtered in rounds
through leaves which are voices
torn from bodies sometime ago

when a kingdom crossed by man
in a day shadows now wither
transit fade moving flowers dawn
longing fast gone ago sometime
archaic dust face down the hero
dead torn from the body voice a
leaf greening now fast pales a
light levered against water a rise
in heat shifts from red to azure
panoply of light drifting from peak
to mountain peak afternoon now
somewhat gone now text riddled
with lacunae to read in what light
remains of day phlox rhododendron
by the side of the footpath leads up
where now just bones tossed random
inflections words soon meaningless
thrown into wind oriented over pools
marginless lotus floating in the center
a god reflected in liquid for an hour
then it is silent light fast phase pale
fading day in a shade briefly before
night falls

05-26-12

(antiphone)

and if I break light this
so much longing no where
once darkened hour revive
to anchor so many books to
then what cannot be against
secret lives plunged in dust
the will of day to fall upon
each a page torn from the light
the flower bed dew spun

each an integer cast from the whole
colder than sleep remembered
rape weed russet grass ichor
who will join to harsh rhyme
through shadowless hades
frost encumbered words
plunge so much longing no
that no awakening inspire
where an anchor indigo deep
if I break and light this
sea of dreams can stranger be
now darkened hour raveling
in her eyes sapphire seems
from a single ray purpose
'neath the bed the tiger growls
or none to go forth the day
for where shades rule none
no more convince this book
the light disdain nor approach
its yellowed pages set against
from hyrcania descend kids
the camera's eye some youth
in whose hands cymbals & incense
retain loud once in bright sun
the veil rent and weeping beauty
that I am here on earth this
underground streams bear her
breaking if I do the light
where ancient sun sleeps hoar
wind and air subtle erasure
on foot or upon a steed blanche
of spoken thoughts cracked
the mirror its innards reveal
glass a mind that ravels thin
whence ire and envy foam green
array of idioms and memory
speaking sure to break sense
round and round the thorn bush
or raving the animal portion tear
to hang a paper to remind who
dreams that blacken certainty
is coming through darkness

but Persephone her shroud white
to this hour of separate planets
treads the simple grass and shoot
how heaves the empyrean its
such confusion and noise about
chest of unlit drawers multiple
does ocean then give birth to night?
spaces in between february and
the gods in their small sickness
april fawn doe hawk and glove
folding in fits fall to earth
all falling down by weighted
for whom grief is a novelty
words to this undone tapestry
as if blind groping for a shape
does night its length display
all things to measure in symmetry
revolving like a maniac image
and orestes still outside the glass
of eyes honey colored once ago
hour of sifting through mown corpses
no more waters rush away
plucking from damask the thistle
bridges cliffs and continents
who hide in cities of rustling silk
crumbling abscess remembrance
oblivious of mind and pattern
this I am light breaking hour
and lie down thumb sucking
jackdaw and spinet music sound
resolve like a firm curtain of rain
in windows convex darkening
come forth then ibis and heron
no other what to ask and pray
devour the body of the text
but aloft on moonbeams love
leave nothing to time's ruin
look my Light! love's discord
nor do battle with chime and frost
always in darkness spent
allay fears of afterlife the ego
this broken hour shadows

crystallizations of heavenly sphere
the dismal souls who wander
no more the skin perceive
eternity dried leaves voiceless
but lie witless in unwinding orbit
myth if I break light this hour
devour still the body of the text
do none of them return
do none of them return

05-28-12

(far)

"This clearly records Ivan S. Pugh born
to Sandra Good on 16th September 1969"
(from Charles Manson and
Joel Pugh – the facts)

the word "ashes"
boulevard of our fathers
to lake Winnebago and back
all afternoon on our tongue
the word "ashes" like sky
a dream in literary sinhala
cause and effect reaching out
when there is nothing
to reach out to admonishment
and ego-function downgraded
to report on exactly how and
why *joel pugh* died
the little boy who wanted
to be a pirate writing backwards
in the mirror in a kensington hotel
decades collapse in a trice
the woman he wanted to marry
but didn't but who nevertheless
took his name in the mojave desert

waiting for history to witness
the birth of still another pugh
is it for us the survivors
to pronounce the word "ash"
to make symbols of the everyday
while in dark corners
chthonic deities deride us?
in what city do we quaff a few
in what remote quarter of memory
where snowbanks flood the sky
do we let childhood escape us
in what distant projection of the screen
do we see ourselves running
from ourselves in a grey despair

But tell me, brother
how is it you finally visited me in dream
arguing quarreling and kissing
standing with me at the pause
to gaze at the famous golden gate
only to fall into a bloody fit
and die before my very eyes?

these and what other scraps of memory
pronounce the word "ash"
while memorizing like venerable bonzes
all the many and more than 25000 verses
of the veda meter and accent intact
is it that we surviving no longer retain
the living water the roiling stream
the embroiled ocean that gives birth
to night?   hooded
vampire women on the prowl
turning the streets to a bloody pulp
sleep deep within us
the photograph of him at graduation
innocent as a just weaned babe
wrapped up a decade or so later
in a comic book fantasy
was for some a murder victim
for others   what
light that circles the vast empyrean

and none for to guide us
none   “ash”
in the mojave desert waiting for “it”
to blow over   the girls

how is it today the rediscovered text
like a forgotten film reel
wavers before the unwary reader’s eye
are there voices as well that narrate
just how the vein splits
or just how to lay the body down
cold on the naked floor
do we turn away
looking for our darkest ghost
do we resolve to sleep
in a bottle of gin
is summer then forever fled?

for james balfour

05-31-12

(endgame)

what finally happened didn’t
the large oval section of night sky
restless intaglios worn by girls
shifting its massive distances
to prove their pubescent sexuality
when morning sounds silent alarms
flirting red-haired with the dead
what finally happened did not
nose insertions navel pins hub caps
a literary work should have consequences
like cats in heat wrecking music
moral imperative powerfully lifted
in the aisles rutting snarling pffft!

to realms namelessly beautiful
torn fishnet stockings spike heels
where breath becomes light itself
nonchalance and dread inspired gaze
were the world itself to die here
sphinx immortal! thou drownest
contusions cerebral lesions seizures
telegraph lunch aspirin pizza binge
echo who can the Ruin of man
been to Samarkand been to Kathmandu
in a single chariot Krishna and Rama
opium the perfume and malt liquor
Shiva and Parvati in the dance
in a trance doing sexual soliloquy
the parking lot as a microcosm
angel rocking against sizzling metal
I saw flame issuing from the ATM machine
wardrobe undress at zero past noon
who no longer have egress to heaven
passing fair between shepherds many
who are denied justice in nullity
known as clusterfuck Dianopolis
and in the used clothing bin the Avatar
the hue and cry arose from the delta
his face a congestion of divine bliss
now come to sit begging for beer
roar of clouds in full serenity
denizens of the ragged underworld
watching in succession mighty gods
the sweet cheat with honey colored eyes
bewilderment and total unconsciousness
strumming a balalaika with her comb
the collapse of galaxies and dust pools
even as pharaoh's corpse glides by
the midden heap of the farthest stars
and the roman centurion cries foul
revolving dynasties of crab nebulae
could care less the red head from Amoeba
immense symphonies six billion years
punk photoclip illusion garbage
few survive to return to the upper world
flipping through pages of the mind

fewer still who recall the journey by boat
hollywood size pictures of genitalia
luminous and radiant the various heavens
said she'd been to the styx and back
and from beyond the far flung archaic
sunflower seeds peyote morning glory
enormous gravel filled driveways leading
the fixed smile of one already long dead
to the mansion on the hill with its tower
shimmying around the fire pole ecstatic
mysterious to this day etruscan haunt

**"also, taking up a load of books from my library to fill
in the book cases; people from Rochester were up last
week to take the Plummer library books, all the dinner
plates , plus the glassware ... all of what came out of the
Plummer House and mother had preserved over the years
... It's sad to go to Rochester with all these memories of mother,
the Vaughn's and all the wonderful times we had together ...
Even more sad to go up north to the house missing Don &
Gertrude! I went to the grave sites on Memorial Day weekend
and said prayers ..."**

and for whom the boatman will have no truck
the missing in action since 1969 without access
the big flirt was nothing but a zombie
vomited in the lap of Anubis
                                                  there
is no way back to the house missing
sad to go   ***with all these memories***
               up north
taking up a load of books from my library
participated in the riots when they burned down
and all the wonderful times we had together
have a deity for each and every household function
people from Rochester were up last week
napalm and agent orange eating up the jungle
she said her name was michelle the zombie
the gods in their intricate illness laying snares
the only man is Krishna everyone else is a woman
playing her one-stringed instrument Mira Bai
I went to the grave sites on Memorial Day weekend
on the sawdust covered basement floor of Larry Blakes
and said prayers ...

and said prayers …

06-02-12

(sand)

this gorgeous day sun washed
that tall tree shaking its green fronds
high in the heraclitean flame
will this ever be the same clouds
scudding their hoary masses
into a horizon of endless azure
temperature at the degree of normal
known as beatitude sinuous meanderings
in the country of the missing musing
on the property of ash spilled
in what unnamed province of heart
down and sleep stunned drifting
away ever away whose remembrance
barely etched in dawn light sifts
through the million portals of time
can still be heard barely a whisper
though all the universes be extinguished
+++++++++++++++++++++++++++++++++
air waves blue vapors transcend
some little property of light diminish
to whom I am addressing this memo
wind fire earth a brief smudge
on the lens a mind a thought aloft
once every a vague lessened water
won't you at least listen to the aztec
who is unwinding within the silver leaf
a rippling through the nearest heaven
drops unending *Tlaloc* curtains of rain
mountains rear their feathery crests
into the tumult of fog and mist
becoming always becoming a distance

soundlessly echoed through the tympanum
where the city sleeps its unfound beast
in the shadow of the pyramid his back
++++++++++++++++++++++++++++++
the house of parrots squalid as ever
mysterious rituals beside the garbage cans
bright color photographs kept away
from the din in a small carved box
with serpent designs *Quetzalcoatl*
secret of fire seeds orange tufted heads
peering through a device near
where the city sleeps its unfound beast
grief without meaning too shifting
through the various keys of time
delta anacreon sappho lucretius
who imaging clear symbols in air
make sense where there is no house
where the door flat open swings
mysteriously over the twenty floors
where there is no one but the small god
of janitors and window washers
is it that we have lost the map
that the way was never the way
+++++++++++++++++++++++
luminous endings luminous *endings*
fictive light embrace wholly tombs
whirling clouds mushroom sounds
endlessly nowhere endlessly *nowhere*
patterns between worlds swirling
down spent flung angels burning
metal struck thunder stroke collides
memory's illusion memory's *illusion*

on a beach somewhere vast of beyond
himself dancing the self's arcane vow
and sand effacing the speaker's voice
and sand effacing the speaker's voice

06-08-12

(listening)

the listening
how far was it
in the azure
terse s i l e n t
evocations of earth
reed huts wattles
between ears
haunted *s i l e n t*
angel in paperback
shining
in sheaths of water
mud indigo a glass
s h a t t e r s music
listening for the soprano
to make sublime the
***to make sublime* energy**
we are nostalgic for
sky tissue cloud warp
a solitary *bee* lush lilacs
smothered in the scent
of silence skin glistens
s w e a t i n g mangrove
afternoons folded within
the very self
a window which was
aloft shadow
of being *of being*
the indeterminate sense
passing from one life to
the next being
light and amaze plural
the dizzy heavens!
a formula for listening
***the* self**
folded within and who
speaks to *that* knowing
language of air
and of fire the seed
green
revolving inside history
until going from
what has ever been *outside*
the boundary burning

and we can listen sprouting
to the tumult *alpha*
without beginning without
from afar longing
to know *longing*
the unknown
in the palm of *her* hand
OMEGA
the stag
the huntress *Diana*
scour the celestial realms for
a sign a signal
that we were born live
futility of cities
making of sounds symbols
for the dead to *speak*
who are among us walking
photographs ruminant
the idea is becoming
from out of the foil of *things*
becoming into ether sheer
transparency l i s t e n i n g
leaves turn in the sun
or torn as a voice
bleeding
becoming *other* which was
hell smoke and ashes
and beyond ether what is?

l i s t e n i n g

06-10-12

(Mansion)

rutilating stones of the heavens,
cliffs …
faith that false abyss …
monument in process

right angles of violent speed
rising ...   curves
around the ...   bends
to peer into the water
suspended by levers above ...
**   whose massive towers**
of dust and pollen reaching
...   double moons
scarlet and   with grief
an inch more and ...   her
possessed by a demon, arching
white ...   basalt hewn
from ...   aztec boulevards,
childhood in plural formations
... winsome face cherubic smile
or buttresses extended ...   clouds
like islands   hidden
in the reeds gods fickle ...
**   their ruses of tin and salt**
how far ...   empty sky
fit incongruently into this patio
... humming   foliage dense
like a text of formulaic language,
nostalgia   in sections
cut out of marble ...   how
many the mannered pastels ...
**   embroidered   ...**
tassels or shreds ...   if there
were a reason for   like
chintz or felt covered ...   her
face blossom-white in the ...
lull darkening forecast the weather
**   sheets of rain   sea a**
lost ...   shape of a
city in despair, incognito ...
the streets in no direction ...
night, imbroglio and loud voices
...   windows of time without
margin   looking out on
the now senseless bay ...   hooded
ornaments, treachery and suspicion
wherever ...   a radio

broadcast announcing
of the dictator …
large ovals pressed into the walls
and for a moment I thought …
dreaming thunder clap
which is … sudden and
coming down in rivulets,
of blood and sand … enormous bull
made of bronze fiery,
using shuttles and lathes … to
obtain the top of the pyramid …
just at the when the rising
sun … many fell
amazed each in place
without any mortar … filed
past in somber array … filaments
incarnadine … who will remember
which deity numbered the planets
moving steadily out, love
its garden abloom with phlox and …
it must have been … heart
regarding the troubadour Rudel,
from afar longing … waves
of impassioned music but
exactly in which quadrant
summer's … weeping
to remember these stones
their positions on the …
a map to be read at eventide
who gather around fondly recalling
the vaughans and the balfours
… circular route leading
up country away from the din
was here the Mansion
was here the
built of sandstone
and carrara … portraits
obliterated, of belief
the perfectly round avenue
each tree carefully planted
to designate now forgotten
was the school …

in winter when the wind
how to keep memory …   how
snows drifting into large piles
nothing more visible …
then going to sleep
sleep

06-13-12

(mountain)

mountain reared half in light
half in infinity
whose hoary tufts
in infinity
I did in a dream erect
what music dawned what
intense energy for a minute filled
is this a waking mind?
what distant fog-shrouded
landscape what unfinished bridge
half in light
celestial fugue
the ever fleeing heavens from our
reach outwards toward what false
eternity
yet round this rooted willow
do shadows measure a course
could we but remain so fixed
did yearning not
false eternity
echoes neither stay grounded
nor in its sparse beauty does grass
move like flame   &   we
breathing imitate what distant planet
beyond our ken this
always

longing to be *other*
and to look out
beneath the mountain reared
half in *light*
the sea *the sea*
such things I think about
mountain tufts fog water
the invisible fire
that makes visible the "all"
our breathing lessens
whitening the distant heaven
which can never be approached
our breathing *lessens*
not the quickened by the light
not the infinite
talking about
the mountain just created
from nothing
and on the other side discussing
Thales and Heraclitus
the one with eyes like fireflies
the other simply on *fire*
the nature and cause of things
discussing the abyss
without faith
the abyss without faith
on this day a "bad air day"
mountain just disappears
and we will talk about
just "that"
dying
celestial fugue
what book
was that in?
like the Buddha preaching
in front of the anthropology library
burning
we are in that book
dying
the conversation turns to salt
to nutmeg ginger turmeric
at each window a sign

which cannot be interpreted
mountain
just *disappears*
forever

06-16-12

(afternoon)

in the event of darkness
taking over in the event
of darkness taking over
it's all right suddenly
the window sashes break
glass silent flies in all
right the suddenly dark
takes in all directions
over in the event glass
shatters silently a dream
is having a cloud burst
event summer usually when
takes over darkening mid
afternoon sleepers drown
clutching to nothing abyss
failure to light the bed
in the event flood waters
break and glass silently
darkens in the tool shed
where the bottle vigilant
waits to be drunk boys
aroused from innocence
to become drunk by mid
afternoon cloud burst is
dreaming darkness in
the event and everything
seems to come to an end
rugs swell darkening near
the twill and scotch bottle

**in the tool shed mid afternoon
sleepy heat stifles everything
dreamers cannot wake boys
drunk swimming in thick
waves no sounds reach ears
burst cloud ahead of time
in the event terrific implosion
drums burst inside ears not
hearing dream within dream
patterns unravel sky work
switches turn off hearing
sensation red shifts darkly
when humid and dank
the room fills invisibly
with uninvited presences
drowned sleepers ghosts
probably in the event who
died darkening afternoons
when lovers collide softly
unaware of the flood gate
eventually everything does
grass fills mouth eyes stare
anodyne sky perplex rhombus
whatever detail a mouth
pronounces late in the day
event of darkness taking
over walls swell rumbling
odd no directions white
until the last hour heat
distinct gods making signs
don't worry fever pitch
boys drunk diving deep
waters all around conscious
of nothing the taking over
event of darkness summer
gods prying make signs
dreamers dying sigh soft
as lovers collide darkening
mouth to mouth heat of
passion taking over
lights flare a single time
fire-flies in the back brain**

names erase names thunder
not heard creases heaven
ages pass in a thimble
darkness over all takes
one by one sleepers who
everywhere are unaware
switches off the fire
moans softly trying to recall
what trying to recall a
single moment in time
when alive was walking
counting clouds swimming
drunk mid afternoon boys
summer thick and green
warm the soft drowning
ears fill water rushes
the ever darkening waters
rushing plunge the body
unawares small gods each
a blade of grass burning
or gravel crunching wheels
someone coming home
in an old black sedan

06-22-12

(charades) ***original version***

cross over the bridge
using both hands and a smile
body and soul the pair
on an old piano roll
the cute girl what's her name
berna **intangible and floating**
above the others in the room
guessing waiting to die
each in turn around a pale

remote thing her name
linda was it she who placed
the score card in my lap
or vomiting out of excess
emotion because a goddess
suddenly took hold of the door
most of them faces
I don't rightly remember
or names spoken in dust
evening wraps its scarf tightly
a chill in the spine going
round wondering what each
gesture each sign each sigh
a breath isolated at the window
a pallor suggestive of spirits
soon night comes with its big car
and who drives it and who
sits in the back seat "necking"
with whom and perfume
sent in circles into the sky
black despite the gush of stars
soon will be going to the dance
holding against the dense dark
the skeleton of choice with
its thick braid of russet hair
and a pair of painted lips
doing the slow step to a song
out of mind and out of time
pyramids most likely
colliding with a great sandstorm
on the edge of town
promise of a future bright
as the carmine colored skirt
death wears on such occasions
taking with her most everybody
who was there playing charades
taking with her of all people
my brother joe

06-23-12

(the bus trip)

some place names :
albert lea mankato winona
red wing austin pine island
stewartville chatfield elgin
potsdam lake city northfield

the word person derives from
eturscan *phersu* mask
dramatis personae who we
were was that really us
packed into an old bus
winding its way to the river
town called red wing a
perhaps reference to a
notable native american
to visit of all things a shoe
factory dense leather smell
tarrying on cobblestone
streets waiting for ice
cream to break the day's
stifling monochrome
school kids doused in dust
screaming chasing hooting
in front of red brick bank
men with green eye shades
windows decorated with
nothing at all german
names associated with
polka music and brass
oompah bands the big
slow moving river just
blocks away carrying
detritus all the way
to gulf of mexico
was it the weather
menacing green thunder
wrecking the syntax
of simplicity turning
sky to a bile colored
was it that already dead

the class of kids loitering
in the heat *bile colored*
the weather smell frying
fish and potatoes thick
small plumes of smoke
from nowhere into clouds
threatening to go home
red wing austin pine island
who like a god driving
the bus its narrow
passage through purgatorio
fields of burnt ochre
ghostly chapels deserted
waiting for a final rain
to drive into mud
the spent corn shocks
waving like souls returned
one more time to
earth's fragile surface
our souls our *phersu*
bloodlessly returning
spent corn shocks waving
at the kids on the bus
who are counting backwards
ninety nine bottles of beer
on the wall *purgatorio*
dense stench of leather
dead animal hides
shoes lined up by the
hundreds waiting for feet
of the dead to walk
-ing to the bus driver
his fragile surface
earthlike skull grinning
beer on his breath
returning his load
of souls to the mayo clinic
perhaps the weather
green bile dark threat
turning the atmosphere
dramatis personae all
into each other's hearts

spent like corn shocks
waving place names
potsdam lake city northfield
somewhere behind the sun
shoe factory a dark
presentiment *breathing*
winding down narrow
passage the bus honking
devils in the rock
abide abandoned chapels
ruins of the soul
or the body politic
clouds glowering a menace
factory puzzled presences
lined up by the hundreds
pairs of brand new
leather dead animals
memory a red brick bank
large plate glass windows
men green eye shades
bald concupiscent drooling
kids on the loose
waiting for ice cream
brass oompah band
"whoopee john and his
six fat Dutchmen"
polkas and schottisches
slanted afternoon light
through fields of dry
corn shocks looking
for the sibyl of cumae
bus releasing carbon
emissions into air threat
baize colored like pool
tables lined up by the
hundreds of them honking
to the mayo clinic
by five in the afternoon
albert lea mankato winona
on the radio it is no time
figures of speech the windows
passing by so fast alarm

barns large as hell holes
wide open and pointless
emptiness all going by
ditches with dank water
animals behind barbed wire
shoes by the hundreds

Persephone is a goddess
being behind a mask
who will take each child
as if it were her own
back below the earth
ere summer is out

06-25-12

(aphrodite)

sappho talked in her sleep to aphrodite

over 2500 years later I saw aphrodite
in a Target store she was wearing
a see-through italian translation
soon she slipped out past the hippodrome
into the city of berkeley in the morning mist
no one recognized the goddess as she headed
straight for the public library
passing on her way the rows of human flotsam
occupying shattuck avenue by the banks
and subway entrance nobody noticed her
sliding in and out of concrete structures
as if they were the void surrounding her
and the days passed like months

if there were a way back to the woods
to the sacred grove   to the temple
where   a sound

headed straight for the public library
where she was accosted in a stairwell
by a man wearing newspaper for eyes
it happened so fast nobody

and the days passed like months

a lunar moth circling and circling
the hydrangeas outside the apartment
the morning silence broken by the siren
of an ambulance going crazy in the fog

lavender   a single bee
from Hybla   and
dressed in a crocus colored

at the subway entrance playing an instrument
called a "syrinx" a man wearing newspaper
for eyes and standing in a pair of elevator shoes
searches his memory
days pass like months

sitting in the midst of the human flotsam
her sex exposed to the concrete
aphrodite   gypsy-hippie-girl
days pass like months

sailed from rhodes to delos and thence
to the cyclades   looking for
the oracle   found hard by the temple
a leopard and in his eyes the promise
of salvation
do not men
keep their word?

days pass like months
a sound

06-26-12

(phantoms etc)

**phantoms ghosts shadows
each of us going in and out
looking for the atlas with the
best coverage of the other world
the one we left behind when
phantoms in the bushes ghosts
prying through brick shadows
moving the wrong way into
hills and dunes and mounds
of darkness matter without
substance moon rock defiles
of purgatory avenues unlit and
desolate as the soul that can
no longer commune with itself
looking for the compass the true
north the evidence of light when
there is only the sound of water
rushing through quartz or sleep
without its divining rod on a
map with no boundaries night
with its demons in pursuit of
the color red or statutory rape
sand rears its immense paragraph
oblivion erases one by one the
streets where childhood unfurled
its multiple mask playing among
trees and lawns where spread
out the panoply of maps awaited gone
our designations and signals
to come to life beside basalt lakes
or green circles of residences
where the gods imitated literature
speaking in classical dialects
to the redundant fates of Beyond
but today is no day at all a blank
on a quadrant of empty space
leaving us nothing but the chill
the enervating glimmer in glass
nothing reflects back no size
of black or distance of azure**

no pinpoints on the road to
nowhere just the marginless
chaos of the pure immaterial
off the chart derailed tossed out
flung damned souls into the abyss
shadows ghosts phantoms
searching for the shape of a hand
for a footprint in damp loam
for a voice an echo a sound
to remember to recall a sobbing
in some hot summer room
hint of perfume wisp of hair
love's stray ephemeral proof
loss grass stained a single leaf
shaking with dew in a silence
caught for a moment in the
have become
a thing
not

06-29-12

(prophet)

how did it come to be
the disciples the crows each
reading the text for what it was
to be right thinking not
deviate from the path
yet either side fallen from
a suggestion is mind is never
the same not in stasis not
in motion a wave frozen
in the long thought it is
always having to be near
the light to be in ascension
to somehow recover what

**was lost in coming into being
that was out of the garden
in the original heat and shapes
like water lifting into the
azure forming and not forming
green and distant at once
to recall what that was before
time's inevitable egg
the face reflected in the pool
or the basalt image cut in the cliff
to imagine that a mind is
talking to its other then
a mask addressing its shadow
somewhere behind the cordillera
that exists massively in a sky
beyond any corollary
bathed in a kind of light
neither lunar nor solar
pyramids hanging huge in night
unobtainable and imprecise
as the stairway that does
not go all the way
as the tunnel that does
not go all the way
and on the street still smoking
his fugitive cigarette the prophet
extends his wish to the soul
even as it passes in myriad forms
through the telegraph of his love
towards some really miraculous
place just outside the city
beyond the framework of reference
and substantiation a shining
a brilliance of eternal dew
that lasts for a second only
when at last nothing comes to be
nor is it explicable
how the prophet miserable
with his fugitive cigarette
goes begging alms unrecognized
even as the sun declares
it is a new day and everything**

will be different starting
right now

06-30-12

(heat wave)

I'm thinking how much it is
to be alive   heat   pornography
threads of electricity   to be
somewhere else or in newsprint
to be read fine   a lens burning
beneath the solar distraction
an avenue with an arm destroyed
totally before the elephant   rubber
humiliation a disgrace   it is to
simply be reading books that take
place in foreign countries   are you
one of them immense and fake   are
you the one about the sewing machine
a girl's tight fitting stocking   so you
can throw away the chintz   albums
behind glass   loan the neighbor
the residual bottle of sauvignon blanc
she won't repay   or it is being rare
solid for a moment   a window looking
out on grass that has yet to be mown
in another story   pornographic
exceptions dying to know   you can
all go to hell   literally this afternoon
you can all go fuck yourselves I don't
care how you do it   in a waste basket
or with a thimble watching the evening
descend   or in a remote part of
the empire where they still spell it
wrong in the hedges   small animals
if not dead already   situations are

dumb white pages with nothing

07-02-12

(talking to the last man)

it's all within you
the back door
the front door
what's that flying in air?
white moth or tissue paper
will this day ever come back?
tall grasses waving tenderly
a hill that accentuates a sky
when the western half is
identical to the eastern half
all within you
yellow specks reddish dots
hallucination invertebrate
contained in a single drop
someone going up country
with his sacks and heavy
footsteps will not come back
will never be as it is
color of hay color of ginger
who will be last to know
what kind is the earth?
is it ever like heaven?
come lie down below this bush
fragrant wild herbs
all within you
listen to the distant water
is it anything like the wells
of heaven?
can we know such things?
soon the moon will emerge
from a thicket of purple clouds

will you be sleeping?

06-15-12

(south)

it's long
how much does it take
out of breath I'm
heading south
lasting for just a
few what does it
take to pass over
to the other side
borderline thin red
a something of dust
cities once there
glimpsed in dream
ice and dew
waterfalls from
nowhere the wayfarer
his shoulder bag
moth worn
what is sleeping
long now and
distance powdery
framed in yellow
disappearing as
everything does
the eye intent on
itself to see beyond
what cannot be
a dream lived
in a library
or in some music
which is always
elsewhere beyond

dust and acres
of darkness rising
nowhere left to
go but sleep
nowhere left to
go but sleep

07-09-12

(natalie wood)

I wanted to marry *natalie wood*
winsome little tart waving the flag
that killed buzz gunderson
we never know the limit of darkness
the beginning of light only
the crazy feeling of being out "there"
nowhere with the enigma
to marry *natalie wood* moving
picture actress ca. 1956 the limit
of darkness the where does it
begin the light we never know
the spiraling condition of being
out "there" crimson suits pill-
box hats perfume lavender spray
something russian about her
raskolnikov in her eyes grim
about to drown without warning
is james dean the true hero
is his skeleton wrapped around a tree
is indiana the only state in the union
is *natalie wood* the only I wanted
to marry is her corpse my dream
lover is her corpse my dream
is only my dream want to marry
imagine mornings in the bath tub
with her a hollywood halo dripping

with suds ivory soap 99% pure
a radio could not be more perfect
a song a picnic splendor in the grass!
"we could have had it all"
is she but a spider a worm an anus
is hers the face of god brooding
on the waters is hers the corpse
drinking 120 proof wood alcohol
in a party to celebrate the king
of sumeria and elul of far dusty reaches
brooding on the waters before light
had a beginning when all dark
the universe was a conjecture only
a radio could not be so perfect
america is a bad nation state
it sleeps on its weapons and rusts
eternally the target of missionaries
it forgets its best movies its murdered
movie actresses its *wrapped around*
***a tree* sending buzz gunderson**
off the cliff the little winsome tart
++++++++++++++++++++++++++
in santa monica it is the end of time
no one is sleeping well
some have dreams of acne and cigars
others remember in dreams only
their marriage to *natalie wood*
and still others have no dreams at all
they are plunging off a solitary cliff
far beyond the dusty reaches of elul
they cannot be invoked as gods
they cannot be worshipped as ancestors
and most will never wake again
fucking and being fucked in a movie lot
where eternity is a painting
where waterfalls made of paper
imitate the heaven of aspirin commercials
where the ghost of *natalie wood*
holds sal mineo's hand as they watch
the gravid and purposeless motions
of the stars

I wanted to marry natalie wood

07-09-12

(folie espagnole)

**comes a time when it's hard
making things mean comes
a time when sense is hard
to find or it's just not there
and you run into an old lover
in the public library one
lazy sunday afternoon
not believing it's possible
or perhaps the gods operate
with magnets drawing
mortals into their music
teasing mortals with their
comes a time when nothing
really matters not the red
kimono not the one possibility
a relapse of history floral
patterns fading listless hours
protracted in text books
about enzymes and catalysts
when nothing means even if
the lover with her beautiful hair
armful of books you kiss her
secretly lazy sunday afternoon
in the public library not renew
old times not rekindle fashions
of love making on mattresses
spread out over bare floors
with music intimating a classical
mythology made remote by
the gods with their magnets**
uselessly rotating in cloud foam

pretending that the plausible
is the real making no sense
of the arbitrary flush of years
ciphers inherited from babylon
when planets were zoomorphs
zero ennui enigma distance
is it because we're frail
is it because we just don't get it
is it because the adventure
is only a footnote in a palimpsest
uselessly rotating in cloud foam
because we just don't get it
we're frail ensnared mortals
caught in indra's net & for
a moment we think to recognize
with her beautiful hair the lover
in the lazy public one sunday
in the afternoon library
trying to get beyond meaning
to get beyond sense into
silence into beyond silence
variations in air and light
at variance with our matter
sheer dross gravity sleep
where are we ever if not outside
the balance outside harmony
in the memory of grass and
wind houses trees small beasts
arrogance to speak of the soul?
going in and out of the Book
consciousness and its deletion
the paranormal and suicide
following the circular avenue
to its logical concussion
in the third floor window
a light flares memory burns
leaves no traces smoke
allure of the remote
her beautiful hair like
a script that cannot

be rightly read
a code

07-14-12

(big sur)

gone
the fugitive poem
gone down the lost
highway some time
gone
ago the fugitive poem
a japanese painting
inside a buick wagon
rushing down cabrillo highway
mountains like dense smoke
surf sky blue crashing
against rock less eternal
than clouds
gone
hazy as manzanita
on scattered stones
around the bend
a tunnel where the dead
we have always known
wait to catch us with
a single word a song
the sound of gas escaping
through the universe
gone
the fugitive poem
like the words of the buddha
about all sentient beings
wheels of the car

making a serpentine sound
hissing on hot pavement
water earth ether
suddenly in a roar
it's all gone the whole world
in a salt evaporator
become invisible
less palpable than light
that seems to lift from matter
the soul in its flimsy
afternoon drapery
gone
a fugitive poem
wordless and distant
about all sentient beings
crystalline diaphanous
the lunacy of night
comes at us
unawares

07-15-12

(llorando)
for naomi watts

if you think that
you were dead already
perhaps it's easier
transfixed in a photo
the day's impossibility
a quandary today looking
for the leaf against
the pane an image
or the double of an image
which is who of the two
hollywood beauties
"I'm in love with you"

dirty t-shirt with nipples
staring at the restaurant
window where it says
orange stays best
bright indelible lips
kiss her soft
kiss her harder
"have you ever done
that before?"
"I don't know"
brooding music dark
the angle suffused from
which night descends
wrapping like a cypress
shadow traces of life
snuffed out
fragments of a text
sectioned off in abysses
and depths monochrome
bordering on red
hysterical meanderings
nocturnal emissions
on crazy street patterns
city of angels veering
off course into sagebrush
ready to burn dreams
pocketed like horoscopes
can you hear me?
didn't get the part
songs ricocheting off glass
partitions mysterious
messages through paper
walls or a corpse
few days old already
secreted into a bungalow
brown with wear
passageways to eternity
necrophilia or nymphomania
buzzing like an insect
in the heart intense
love as it can only be
"out of my mind"

dionysian symbology
in an underworld created
by pornographers
and drunk cineastes
zigzagging gods no larger
than midges devouring
a blade of grass
or just staring into
a reversible mirror
the mask of envy
++++++++++++++
if we are given
only a day to live
would it play out like this
dusty past midnight
in a mexican theater
where everything is
tape recorded
an illusion even waking
hallucinatory in blond
wigs and carmine lipstick
watching the singer
with painted tears
gilded and tragic
collapse on stage
though the song
goes on and on
into the ether
llorando por tu amor
on and
                on
into the
                                    ether
would it play
                            out
like this

silencio

07-20-12

(dark knight)

**key lock rust bronze
bees bougainvillea time
how much in an instant
surpasses already the past
a mind elevated attuned
abashed a goddess at
the door ready to vomit
fate youth elongated into
what matters a mostly
diatribe against passing
done with finished a while
white bleak blank black
a book pages pasted
to poems unread rewritten
squandered in bad light
fulminated by some un-
heroic deed fumbling for
keys smith drained tool
plied flanks smoothed
ties tide vast empyrean
flushed empty
sitting in a strait jacket
talking to the moon
mother god angel
demon behind bars
drinking steam switch off
girl-boys too pretty dahlias
back-ended her moaning
snake charm spittle dip
parenthetical birth stone
worn hip wise slender
as lotus stem azure blue
indigo lavender kisses
lips sewn french style**

to whom it may concern
piano strut players die
tossing into the foam
eternal girdle aphrodisiac
movie theater massacre
newsbits around clock
section about neuralgia
cure vegetating reddens
tight clasp swollen sex
a hit followed by many
more hits

07-22-12

(houses)

houses houses lined up houses
some speaking dialect some in pure
up and down the remembered street
trees lining houses green remembered
children houses dolls broken green
remembered lined up summers long
frozen mirrored lined up houses
haunted emptied houses gone long
summers speaking dialect others
studied latin greek furniture dusted
lined in rows to eye's end frozen
books of houses books more books
maps where houses lined up streets
imaginary maps of houses where streets
lined up or in curves circular bending
descending to harbors ascending
to hilltops malls and lawns and cemeteries
where houses lie on houses for ages
summers gone behind houses green
foraging hillsides houses worn emptied
haunted brooding dark crevices houses

**abysses distances longing windows
rain sleet hail snow sunshine designs
patterns in dialect or pure houses
shining or not shining white board
shingle roof tile slate grey marble court
houses like castles tudor houses mansions
libraries houses of books maps documents
parchment signals waving high houses
flags staffed with slaves houses servants
quarters domiciles outhouses frozen links
to historical chambers portraits of houses
lined up in rows of unnamed streets houses
behind houses in front of houses sideways
stargazing houses verandahs grand lodges
bullets arrows slings unfinished houses
ditches sloughs canals ringing houses
cities like houses of cities ancient houses
enormous memories of houses palaces
skies even with houses clustered like
dynasties of solar systems and galaxies
houses with gods chattering at dinnertime
or goddesses irreverent having sex in beds
the size of ink houses remotely like caves
houses full of enemies in circular rows
going round and round night time houses
musical houses ghostly shrouded houses
many more houses out of sight suburbs
of houses houses of suburbs maps of suburbs
that have yet to be maps inside maps
maps unfolded on lawns of houses memories
memories of houses children parties
in houses maps unfolded or drawn on walls
showing still more maps within and without
strange sounds seeping through houses
spirits in decay ancestors dying again
wanting houses back wanting houses again
to die again in the right house this time
or no time at all houses rows of them
endlessly making of memory a vast house
stairs going nowhere attics basements
coal shoots slumber rooms rugs worn
burnt floor boards winsome tapestry**

woven carpets persian delicacies death
behind the walls death below the floors
death in the guest room houses death
houses elevators unfinished smoke
parlors tea cups ashtrays houses of
infinitely losing memory infinitely
escaping through holes in the sky
heavens houses of heavens disappearing
eternally gone houses without shape
summers fading green without a trace
streets winding up in sand dust abysses
houses tossed off cliffs waters wailing
waves awash with houses memories
disappearing hold on to nothing
steps here and there sandboxes wood
chrome helium everything suddenly red
eye out of context seeing instead
of houses the long angel of Beyond
hands wrapped in curtains sobbing
muffled houses crashing in on houses
afternoons more afternoons evening
when there are no more houses
distances with a flash of tinsel
houses echoes of houses echoes
darkness fading itself out of
lined up places empty
syntax shot
words
hiss
the
a

07-24-12

(senex)

**how little we need to say
how much we over speak
sky is once enough to see
a hundred years the same
then off to die alone again
mums gladiolus morning glory
bright as clouds that drive
into abodes of secret gods
of envy lust and treachery
is heaven never near
is hell this place between
the ears the mind's shaft
abyss of tangled thoughts
to speak clearly in time
just once to speak as if
to ancients in their dialect
what's true what's good
as water pure pouring
from the mountain spring
and need no more to pine
what's lost what never was
geese make alphabets
pacing the northern sky
crows execute paragraphs
in great gusts of wind
the corn lies cheated
on frozen ground unsought
when will in dreams
the beloved come back
when does youth ever
acquit itself of distance?**

08-04-12

(from the *pali canon*)

the little man from sri lanka
has a lot to do today
get passports in order
durable power of attorney
figured out
put friend to rest
on hill slopes great tea plantations
ready to burn under tropic light
to rest
friend dying of unknown
and sepsis sets in
to remember the words of the
buddham saranam gacchami
last things in order
to rest
farther north tamil tigers
waiting to resurrect
under fierce tropical sun
australo-dravidian dialects
retroflex consonants and clicks
humming in the weird grasses
insects with saucer size eyes
or petty deities gnawing on air
to rest
large fans turning slowly
on the plantation house ceilings
planters punch or ice tea
on the verandah
ghosts of british colonials
living in denial or put
to rest
the little man from sri lanka
hurries in a blur of karma
setting this here
setting that there
buddham saranam gacchami
friend dying of terminal
to be flown by medical transport

to nirvana
to rest

08-06-12

(this land)

what did the sikh
do to the america?
what did the america
do to the sikh?
guns boom boom don't
kill people do
kill sikhs the america
its gun loaded big hunt
love game and gambling
buck stag roped across car
big man trusses shot
put in sights anything
the america loves shoot
the sikh comes from amritsar
where the golden temple is
the sikh goes to oak creek
in the green state of wisconsin
why do the sikh leave
his golden temple
what do the sikh
in blue turban and thick beard
believe in
do we know
is it christ is it krishna
it is One Immortal Being
the brotherhood of man
the america don't believe

the america has right
to bear arms
the america goes on the hunt
lunatic macho trigger happy
the america don't believe
it has manifest destiny
to bear arms
to bring democracy to the world
to shoot 'em up
in schools movie theaters
and sikh temple
clouds of purple majesty
waving fields of golden grain
betsy ross blind in both eyes
fathers of the constitution
huddled in B'nai B'rith
plotting to kill Algonquin
iroquois winnebago ojibway
with automatic weapons
the sikh has a dagger
guru nanak flowing white beard
preaching purity
god has no features
there are no avatars
who is the sikh
that the america wants to kill
is he terrorist because of turban
yes he is the other
come to live in oak creek
but he uses cell phone
just like you or I
he speaks english the sikh
filthy wogs
the sikh is your friendly
cab driver who wants
independence for the punjab
brotherhood of man
clouds of purple majesty
amber waves of grain
this land is your land

08-07-12

(two small poems)

i

**the masters
counsel silence**

**when fireflies tick
in the warm night air**

**when cherry blossoms
drown in untimely snow**

**when the empty pillow
attests to the heart's pain**

**when from the drawbridge
the poet plunges inebriate**

**did no one teach him
when to stop singing?**

ii

**what passes for time is
just an echo in the dream
of water passing through night
a stretch of the imagination
one day passes all days pass
there is in the numen at the top
of the stairs a small inscrutable
destiny before the waking eye
put the finger in the grass
to find the broken half
lean the head to the side
the mirror returns nothing
of its memory
together shadow**

and substance morph into
nothingness

for jack foley on his 72nd

08-08-12

(au revoir)

saying goodbye saying to a son
goodbye saying over and over
to a son goodbye saying goodbye
over goodbye and goodbye
over again to a son to a son
how many times in a lifetime
soon the paper wears thin
tears goodbye saying color
fades ghost takes over a grassy
knoll flying a kite goodbye
to that to the flying a goodbye
again and over the airplane
is soon lost in some siamese
heaven sometimes a jungle
intrudes or the desert saying
over to a son goodbye the air
seems to part a weave a shift
in tone and red brighter than
the sun this afternoon goodbye
to overwhelmed that a lifetime
has occurred so suddenly just a
minute ago at the toy store and
goodbye to a siamese heaven to
a desert now to a famous city
without a name a lifetime is
over again and goodbye to
the eye dry from dreaming
a son remember so long a lifetime

**ago rubbing against a chalk
wall in italy or the break in time
the eye dry from sleep the color
of sand of a funnel of ants reaching
into the sky where the airplane
comes to rest for an infinity
is only an afternoon was here
and is gone so goodbye and again
over to a son en route to who
knows where heaven drizzles
a fiction of faces passing so
fast it doesn't matter married
and with children behind glass
isn't it reaching over the top
isn't the kite lost now in a closet
isn't dust and whorls of something
yellow and incandescent in sleep
only a hand fast fading a goodbye
to once again to never maybe
writing the algebra of the stars
fast becoming night**

08-22-12

(sleeping madonna)

**in the book I wrote you are
reading the book I revealed
where you never sleep being
gilded ornament of pornography
it says you are to be abjured
cursed fluxed blasted ruined
cruising like jet stream dreams**
god of rivers! god of sleep!
**the little lulu of sex I wrote
being obsessed crazed nuts
in the book you read which**

I wrote about everything I
could think about you but
sleeping now adolescence
teen angel metallic hubba hubba
somnolent black and white
poster paper rippling inside
dementia and angst and folly
the book I mean I wrote
you could never be reading
archaic demon-script chisels
notching flesh entries for
every vocabulary item I chose
for your identity sleeping
idiomatic downgrading slender
chance to write like that
again the puzzling enigmatic
lack of reason purloined ideas
thankless task of writing
automatically morning after
blessed morning in dawn
of time forsaken by policy
nuanced in the diatribe
of pornographic simulation
all fiction is there in godhead
fundamentally destroyed
in order to be understood
skin flashes portfolio meat
zippered unzippered female
sex organs menacing and wet
there is a light above your head
madness becomes electric
overdose fulminated meth-head
trooping topanga canyon for
just a glimpse flexing your
small adipose in a daydream
god of rivers! god of sleep!
you are always reading into
whatever book has no covers
dust jacket ejaculated movie
what no civilized mind would
chitter chatter cocktail talk
late afternoons in the universe

fated star dazed asleep dumped
into a photograph of the recent
past black and white orgasm
with subject in repose slightly
far to the right of the black hole
pages and pages of transylvanian
folk lyrics green apple leaf
autumn term nostalgia longing
enigma forever uncoded minoan
script baffling over mouth
french kissing a plaster deity
all mythography in that sealed
labial misunderstanding cloudy
always reading that over and
over page at the footnote bottom
top ended for alley junk
description of the "other" for
once and all sublimely slept
twixt pages of glossy magazine
in iota subscript about greek
religion shards wings totem deities
arrested without warrant for
public indecency of the highest
order pointing to already
dead asterism in symposium
please pass the grape juice
between parentheses naked
put to sleep by the veterinarian
your once blond mass of hair
tainted and tinted oxided
beyond repair afloat like rust
in a farthest galaxy namelessly
rutilating and ancient fragments
sapphic verse in oceanic
delusion   tantric
god of rivers! god of sleep!
the negative of the your self
backwards read in a book
of lost flights down swung
in sleepless antipathy of worlds
naked processed skin "words"
I meant negatively associated

with superlative hiatus
known as time between we
are born and die submerged
in fantasy entelechy "amore"
looking restlessly for elusive
photo encompassing all symbols
in a single shot flesh and
whorls of yellow distemper
rushing through grassy fields
to no known end asleep
caught in a montage frozen
like the song somehow
observed chiaroscuro ellipse
a kiss followed the thousand
catullan others labia dis-
membered starstruck pantheon
darkness chill skin coming
undone in biblical passage
can never get at the root
at the why at the because
some kind of etruscan house
god fused like metal to sun
interpreting hermetic inroads
to the massive house of sleep
sand colored maze of ants
reconstructing their own sky
somewhere behind your lids
red followed by stairs
cheap and immense and
like small islands afloat
disconnect pathology sweat
reading and rereading the
part about the part about
cannot remember distinctly
lexicology of dismemberment
osiris for lunch on via veneto
god of rivers! god of sleep!
in a grain substantially dry
heavens collide
            the eye asleep in its
kaleidoscope

08-29-12

(labyrinth)

after all this time it still
doesn't feel right I mean your
total absence your disappearance
half the planet remains darkened
as do so many other astral
projections the kind you played
with using numerical abstractions
as if they were toys of the mind
beyond anything else the sound
of your voice is missing when I
answer the phone knowing full
well that somewhere else in
a pastoral fourth dimension
it goes on talking just like me
in and out of the labyrinth
the one created by daedalus
under a blazing cretan sun so far
back in time when lawns could
be lifted neatly into the sky and
angels without physical properties
accompanied us to the movies
in and out of the labyrinth
fading back to that other logos
speaking in perfect hexameter
falling back between pastures
where mythological creatures roamed
wearing our masks for faces and
reciting the great poetry of nostalgia
known only to those who understand
the color of rain and dust
it isn't for that I am crying today
not for the cloudless hemisphere
that aches with a terse subjunctive
not for the trees along the way

that are yearning for the endless
in and out of the labyrinth
is it night where your formless
is it darkest yet where your formless
what is it I am about to cry
jazz muted in the absent ear
the untranslatable shouts of children
a block away in home town
almost sunset and shadows elongated
bicycle between the small hills
in search of the missing back door
in and out of the labyrinth
untranslatable shouts of children
I am about to cry

09-01-12

(mud)

"je redeviens mortel"
s. beckett

I become mortal again again
as if never before mortal and
singing in the mud just below
eye level green where it turns
into a different season a divine
loss the thread of time a thin
flue of saliva borne on the wind
this time as never again before
it goes out like breath fleeing
the wounded mouth like a light
extinguished by some god's
opaque desire to never again
let this happen if it has a name
in mud in silence approaching
a house on the other side of the

hill the invisible one the house
darker than before or again
silence troubling the small pane
of glass rippling dew on the leaf
whatever it was going out the lamp
its flame sputtering nightwards
again or the sound of time more
like a hissing on the anvil distant
whenever that was a second or two
before everything else goes out quiet
remorse dank sections falling off
into the water somewhere below
presentiment of meat and conscience
however that comes about a brief
wasn't that long ago if it seems so
or when it can still be seen at eye level
above the mud and silence above
the hill opposite time beyond the house
the invisible one where the singing
was where the noise of speech and
crying of children was the dim focus
when it was mortal and teasing a
small god where sections falling
the roof holes raining through an
epoch of bitter lees going out like
a flame somewhere in the house
the invisible falling off dark sections
a remnant being mortal in the eye
glass a view from behind raining
already the intricate deity of sand
fixing sleep with a color more like
beyond what lies darning socks
in the dark blindly overture to time
brass muted horns a dusty farewell
to virtually everything it was called
"brother" once when it becomes
mortal again I on the chance listening
for the post to slip under the door
or evacuating the attic of its ghosts
trying to remember which summer
that was where the sidewalk bends
for the tree growing out of proportion

as so many things do not understanding
never the will to become immortal
just once outside the day's small limb
falling outside the window into grass
where a myth of humans cast to sea
makes music almost silent in the mud
below which something else sleeps

09-17-12

(a mystery)

the other side of the door
a mirror dust a chasm
who will not appear again
lost in the mid afternoon heat
the things we could not discern
the countries landscapes quarries
boroughs sandwiched between
vast hills of sleep dun colored
wastes just beyond the border
who cannot appear again
among these sundries a glass
inverted to make the moon
even closer to the minute
or a smaller deity still advancing
on its blade of grass to hail
the now fragmenting light
so many times ago a lesson
bitterly taken you on one side
of the door and the Other coming
to meet you on the edge
wavering like a mirage
shimmering for all the world
to disintegrate in the palm of
your hand or the Other at once
upon you seizing your shadow

who has disappeared for sure
in the tangle of undergrowth
just behind the garage where
the gooseberries grew

09-19-12

(psychoanalysis)

this is the mayo clinic
these are the great brass portals
of the mayo clinic
this is the x-ray chamber
of the mayo clinic
and this is the butterfly in the brain
of the mayo clinic
this is no longer a childhood
yet I am brought to tears
by the block of stone
that rests at the foot of the bed
I am disturbed by the so many
memories
that do not correspond to the sack
of dandelions
picked at the crossroads in may
and am not convinced that the
dream of reason
fits into the left-hand glove
translation of the unreal omegas!
spotless the great sand-colored library!
where the county jail once stood
a ring of gopis
surrounding the lotus-born one
in which world do I wake?
all the so-called friends are dispersed
in yellow dust
such are the ruins of melancholy

and nostalgia
and the tavern where poetry reigned
a gasoline station
a fiction in the glass of passing time
when am I ever myself?
this is the marble labyrinth in winter
of the mayo clinic
this is the mysterious rhyming carillon
of the mayo clinic
so many afternoons in a single moment
collapsed in grass
am I transported to the dance?
is this the inevitable pharmaceutical
darkness alone?
it keeps lingering in a cherry coke
it keeps waiting for the snow to end
it keeps buzzing the green summer heralds
this is everything tumbling out of the dryer
no one cares any more about the granite
about the aimlessly drifting sky
about the river underneath the mall
no one understands about the
maybe it's because I'm depressed
and angry and lonely diminished
and marginalized forgotten loony
a drained river bed of illusions phased
out stuck here in a lightless basement
smelling long years of urine and paraffin
listening listening for the mayo clinic
for the you know how it is when
afternoons so many collapsed
into a single blade of situationism
when you yourself can't understand
who you are why I am intact
but wounded mistaking almost everything
for something else it's called symbolism
it's a rat's nest of passion
bitterly recalled it's more like
I don't know maybe masturbation
truncated isolated unable to finish a
single verse rambling instead to the wall
a mattress in disguise chimes ringing

inevitable drugstore date with freckles
mooning over an incomplete sandwich
or a song a piece of music stuck
in the mayo clinic yes in the mayo clinic
already way past the hour
already who hasn't felt
an itch in the middle of the night
holding on to nothing the silent
amaze a beast with kind eyes
just staring into the
going up and down in the grand elevator
                    of the mayo clinic
guessing what each patient has
some terrible incurable life
a disease they brought from the old
is it because I speak mexican?
axolotl mescalin popocatapetl peyote
to remember the floating gardens
to recall dimly the mansion in san angel
to have been part of a half
a shadow on a map being drawn
over and over a large yellow sheet
or winter again icicles and frozen laundry
shifting in the cold nothingness
anti-american
this is no longer a childhood

09-28-12

(ezra)

climbing
between chaste slates
of gray waves
stone weaving through
stone pumice
and cordial color

of october sky
meandering archaic
through verse
half rhymed
partially erased
cavalcanti and Alcaeus
hooded remnants
peering through dazzle
of rain and pharmacy
tardy neon
of the last century
pattern making
on the steep slopes
of umbrian gubbio
and from afar
the haunted shrieks
of swallows diving
in the abyss

10-02-12

(autumn leaves)

sky a perfect blue so terse
leaves falling in sun wash
everything is lived in this
very instant of flowers and
reflections   nobody
is really alive and the breath
that inheres is a thing
of the past like songs once
heard captured by memory
that somehow survive
in an unimaginable future
we are not there we are not
anywhere at all unless
it is in the instamatic

your terrible hungover breath
at the same time elucidating
the concise math of the spheres
stars whose suddenness
is at once their demise
everything echoing echoing
forever in this irreducible
moment of perfect azure
leaves effortlessly falling
sun wash making invisible
the countless bodies
passing by going absolutely
nowhere

10-06-12

(the difficulties)

> *"see the marketplace in old algiers*
> *send me photographs and souvenirs"*

an enormous female deity composed
entirely of dust obstructs the front door
another one with her intensity of sand
sifts the little light that shows through
the mind's vacancies called living
a memory of white arms shining
a photograph with its fading actors
as if expecting still another female deity
this one made up of cosmetics and pearl
to remove from the air a false history
of alabaster and the siege of ants
a memory of white arms shining
who are the enemy if not the ones
dwelling within all red and bright
to develop the day's quick saliva
"this isn't everything that we are

these silly dream puffed up ornaments"
φλεγεθον   ληθη   στυξ
and at the exit an inscrutable divinity
with a sword of burning air held aloft
choosing not to bear shape or substance
who commands and essentially destroys
whatever was here before in spirit
and form us the groveling and spitting
a memory of white arms shining
is it to prefer pornography to virtue
holding in the eye a brief passing moment
the ineluctable goddess of transience
whose impossible beauty renders mad
all and sundry panting and barking
on all fours lewd dogs we are become
and have not to sate us the porous sponge
"come hither Tityrus with thine oaten reed"
hunh? the enigmatic and yet unwholesome
past-time it is living in the instamatic
revolving between photos of what was
and what could be insane projectiles
with talking mouths sput- sput- sputtering
ah! the inane and empty dialogue
between mathematics and repentance
taking place in the midnight kitchen
each of us masques in orange and pink
what is best forgotten resurfaces time
and time again and to the breast is pinned
the sacred heart target of the immense
and feminine deity of the crossroads
whose sheer physical presence is a threat
we never come to fully understand
a memory of white arms shining
how it can never
how it can never return
how it can never return us
how it can never return us to
how it can never return us to what
how it can never return us to what we
how it can never return us to what we were
φλεγεθον   ληθη   στυξ

10-09-12

(poetry)

**a small hill divided unequally
or a hand shifting from right to red
lengthening shadows of brothers
intimating a sunglow of catastrophes
because no one is really listening
as the page a huge white sheet
carelessly unfolds beneath the lake
and words effortlessly emerge
largely unrecognizable like madonnas
lined up in a vast marble quarry
which could have meaning and sound
as well chiseled moments of thought
and feeling pausing to take water
by invisible paragraphs into the azure
where clouds assume magnificent poses
becoming isolated and nostalgic
wanting to turn into island meadows
where heroes forage for their souls
such dusty monuments of the arcane
how do such moments transcend
even the most intricate paths of sleep
and to summon from the depths
the impossible translations of the "other"
pronouncing from left to green
hypothetical syllables an epic of and
beyond adolescent yearnings
but to fall suddenly like a curtain of sand
into the labyrinth of misunderstanding
to sound the abyss searching asking
for the portal the ivory gate the airy
distance where the library stands
a mirage shimmering in its autumn
of timeless knowledge the unapproachable
and from all the various meanings**

to derive the One and remain stunned
like bees in winter watching black
and white the endless film revolve
page after page of the empty and void
++++++++++++++++++++++++++++
how is it that yesterday there was
no trace of our narrow existence
and tomorrow   what?
was the focus byzantium?
at the surface only the song remains
there is a fragment   drums
"why the two brothers were quarreling"
"why the map did not unfold at all"
"why next to the origin of red a small deity"
"next to nothing there is a film loop"
"tomorrow is the place of unknown"
"shadows not men   "
take up arms against the myrmidons
from afar   scent of rose water
something   in the wind
islands adrift in the sun   distant
as an unremembered childhood dream
as an unrecalled   swift
to the earth the felled body
between the ears running a lamp
gone out
++++++++++++++++++++++++
take the hand and learn to write
a garbled sense at first
at the margins small images
to remember everything now and
put it down in ideograms
tiny chalk nubs   a garden
the mind
first was here a thing unshaped
fear   or the dozen shades of light
upon the sun's return

inches away from death

"shadows not men   "

10-11-12

(habibi)

"je nous sais tous ici ..."
s. beckett

eternity and jade endless summer
destruction of world systems
spinning on the buddha's fingertip
music that suddenly rushes out
from under the door a sound riot
stripping the mind of any causality
you wanna go crazy watching her
perform the legendary blues number
(*euthyphro kratylos gorgias* in love
with Alkibiades stoned at the bar
surrounded by his turkish houris
unmindful that a life has run out
sleep the size of sand envelopes him)

wordless dreams erase one by one
the countless syllables of the epic
it is a function of red anticipated in
the echo reverberation of her mouth
lapse in space small lights extinguished
planets running around like mad dogs
in the eventual collapse of everything
woven in and out of the blues number
moon faces peer wearily through smoke
each cigarette is a deathless god

"I want you to rock me Baby
like my back ain't got no bone"

the pleiades seven in number illustrate
a child's idea of the sky at night
everywhere in the tavern faces turn
toward the appearance of the Prophet
doors open effortlessly windows darken

drinks come and go in the wink of an eye
love wearing the nothing of a day on trial
weaves the sylph of her self in sawdust
ready to give herself to the Prophet
who is at once manifest and annihilated

saliva grass crickets nightfall death

para ximena monzón

10-15-12

(personae)

(i)

manifest in our absences
we provoke shadows somber
in review of our non-actions
swinging from green to left
in some ethereal dream
where time lacks corners
in our absences manifest
long afternoons of foliage
turned to rust and mulch
a moment to love suddenly
stolen from the mirror
now fogged over and unsure
this winter will be final
assumes the blade of grass
balancing the delicate god
who presides over absences
ours and yours as well
tottering over the great abyss
where in folds less and less
distinct our various presences
are buried in smoke and ice

never was much for expression
pushing the self into its corner
looking for a window for a
never mind the hullabaloo
of the world outside a riot
of color and sound dreamt
ever unreal of the imagination
the always unkempt wildness
of the unbridled mind
pressing into an absence
the hundred thousand voices
it projected thinking it a life
shadows tombs heavens that
simply are not there

(ii)

does anyone ever come home?
for loss of meaning when does it?
entrenched in his half-mind
the imperfect deity of memory
resolves to never again corrupt
air with his absence and yet
we are sent into breathing
attached to senseless names
to the abstraction of meat
some of us wearing hair for beauty
others angry for lack of it
what can come of this thrill?
the many are on the wrong path
trees and immense mountains
make myth of their error
it is only distance and its map
of invisibility and nightfall
to the right of the conjunction
the severed hand of syntax
conducts the clouds of thought
yet we are never any closer
and the river that endlessly circles
gives fire to the combustible mind
and still we are never nearer
to the immense memory we lost

passing from one life to the next

10-26-12

(poem from the unfathomable
Ur-Text)

when you meet her going to school
what season is it all blossom singing
sun in its house of sparkling glass
and wind shaking the invisible world
as if whatever it takes she should be
yours alone powerful and beautiful
in her archaic fundament of tresses
wet from the underground recess
the last half year in hell with mother
but now like Diana springing deadly
with her bow and quiver alert
to the hunt to spill some stag's blood
sprinkling with gore innocent grass
can you hold her for a moment only
without yourself dying hear the sirens'
whining pitch as you fall from grace
reciting out of a dream the spell
darkness woven in her very kiss
you shouldn't have done that No
picking your shadow up from stone
a cold brace of unintelligible words
sudden-
ly
dizzy
are you aloft
winging with the osprey
or merely stunned in the circular
ruins of time?

10-28-12

(quetzalcoatl 2012)

this is my *mansion* she sd
but I'm not *joe* I told her
invited me to enter her dark
immense sections of time
the color of fading grass
and a swarm of small deities
the size of mosquitoes
it was happening quite fast
she moved between & through
massive blocks of stone
she moved as if a planet
grazing the citadels of light
in its passage to nowhere
my *mansion* she sd
not *joe* I told her quite
fast it was happening she
moved through massive
planets of and through stone
fallen in the hegemonies of angels
who can hear me in all that
din enter she invited me
like fading grass sections
of time immense in ruins
going round the absences
a galactic mystery that surface
suddenly like milk in touch
the thousand and many deities
smaller than mosquitoes
in a swarm descending
on the lawn where prone we
observed the massive constellations
enjoy the summer of their
essences that once inhabited
a place called zumbro falls

not far from the entrance to hell
where a mendicant achilles
waits his turn she sd
not *joe* with large sad eyes
set in a distinctly mexican face
my *mansion* she sd in a sort
of journalese with a camera
above her left hip shaking
ever so slightly the invisible
worlds manifest in her eyes
gods with abrupt names and
a hawk-like nose climbed
the pyramid of the sun
it was 1953 air like quartz
shimmering near the entrance
to hell that small ditch
just behind the filling station
on the highway to zumbro falls
she sd hitchhiking in a
loose summer frock bare
shouldered like an egyptian
in her tiny boat weaving
through time's immense
corridors sandy stretches
of sleep and nostalgia
set in a distinctly mexican face
his large sad eyes she sd
my *mansion* the labyrinth
who can follow me can never
return the same she sd
then there were a lot of Aztec
words not easy to translate
some one with a shining machete
stalking through fields of maize
in the autumn of her shoulders
bare hitchhiking to zumbro falls
with achilles dead drunk
the riot of light behind
the filling station where they
load the corpses fallen
among hegemonies of angels
can see how blood gathers

forming a map of consciousness
for a brief moment only
hieratic and dizzying
stu- stu- stuttering in aztec
polyphony sad large eyes
in a distinctly mexican face
I'm not *joe*
my *mansion* the labyrinth
she sd

10-28-12

(dia de los mue- mue- mue- muertos)

hapax legomenon! charlie chan!
side stepping globe trotting side
by side with syd vicious punk hole
all hell in her waist little lulu!
if I could rename her nancy
or caroline or martha dooby
dooby doo I certainly would
but she's always gonna be catrina
la muerta de acapulco jail bait
zombie who sings trio los pancho
perfidia bolero and besame mucho
man she is the orgone box *plus*
moving right to left the ghouls
in question masked as humans
demand civil rights before certain
death & with fists full of sky tear
the paper palaces to shreds
howling insanely about the time
angel got it like agamemnon
but hey is that joe in their midst
wearing his high school band
uniform red and grey oom pah
he's heading straight for lulu

bang up time in the shrubbery
bo diddly doing the cake walk
and singing “bring it to jerome”
it’s like feast day at saint lourdes
all the dead raking leaves and
shoving detritus in the gooseberries
a romp drinking gramps’ dandelion
wine and clouds coming somber
through all the windows and joe
huffing and puffing his eyes glassed
he’s *seen* the gospel truth something
like a hundred million galaxies
exploding all at once right behind
the garage where the whetstone stood
brightly spangled mariachi band
strikes up “la virgin de la macarena”
wild eyed werewolf hip hop bounce
abracadabra corpses lined up
on south broadway for extreme
OM SHANTI OM
unction with joe in the middle
waiting for his communion wine
on his knees all pitiful head wobbling
round and round the day has to end
the day has to end the day has to

11-02-12

RESPONSE

for philip lamantia

how can I miss you now that you’ve stepped into Mt Aetna
like a bare-armed Zavuyan surfer
more like a blade of grass than a wired green stiletto
you with your egyptian book of the Living Dead
with your tourist trap ticket to Mare Mortuum

**with your lunar baedekker aspirin field fuzz
mounting like a caravanserai over the outback of Testosterone
thinking all the while to be an innocent in the American Cafe
where columbus avenue intersects the planet Dorothy Lamour
miss you? sniffing breeder of post havoc doggerel suspense
a rhymester cloaked in high school gad-about spectacles
and a judgment mouth long on hari krishna syllables
who never learned the lesson of integral cloud physics
miss you? with your cable car disease four furlongs deep
when chinatown takes a dive into the ambrosian morph
when the dial-a-murder mafia types strike up a pose
looking more glamorous than marilyn dead
when the big frisco hotels with their railroad barons
burn to a crisp like a five hundred page illegible novel
the one that describes the rebirth of anna karenina
in the oval tent of the endless presidential campaign
giving egg to the shanty trodden homeless t'ang dynasty poets
no way miss you and your comuniqués to max ernst
all about the european transvestite rain forest
you already mist of the mists above the thousand mountains
of a lost silk screen painting where love extended
like an angel above the ravages of mars
simply disappears stroke by livid stroke**

11-04-12

(junk)

**I told you not to go there
the brakes never got fixed
it's too early to go to sleep
she was no good from the start
hunting in her purple buskins
like she was some kind of goddess
doesn't help to stand around moping
it's cocktail time in the plaza
why didn't you listen to me**

why did you have to keep on wearing
that beat up old orestes mask
by nightfall the waves should be
pounding the cliffs deaf
the moon will be at her brightest
and still you insist on your rights
aztec dream thunder in both ears
helium time in the cancer ward
and by noon all the fangs out prowling
looking for rain nymphs and dwarf stars
but you wouldn't listen to me, hunh?
jack diving into pure bread fruit
native minstrelsy breeding fear
and suspicion while los angeles fries
on its own tropic of capricorn
pachucos devil buzzing in the imported sky
of cellophane wrap around christmas
you could hardly wait to listen
to her ovaries concluding a pact with time
dread roses swarming near tokyo
private fireflies engrossed in death-watch
everything becoming circular
nasty sound track in the teenage nightmare
more than one chainsaw working at a time
hour's up when you could have had
a lick at the jesus freak
pasted out on the sidewalk beside
the living barking dog-alike
heaven simply disintegrates like confetti
over the automobile cemetery
where you and girlfriend have it out
masturbating like dead angels
between one concrete life and the next
it's to come back from the dead
it's to return morphed as prophet isaiah
it's to shift from one red star to another
junk days in old romeo town
or straddled on the peyote rooftop
playing the charlie parker saxophone
though there's nothing in your hands
and you take the nose dive
into the concerto grosso sidewalk

is this some kind of buddha trap?
I told you not to go there
I told you not to go there

11-06-12

(saturday)

why add to the already limitlessly
decomposing pile of countless poems
contributed this year alone?

I'm with you, bro'
sky is an imperfect paradise
replete with invisible complexities
as is this poem dedicated
to the late t'ang dynasty bards
many of whom remain nameless
despite yes the great autumnal avenues
that fairly adumbrate with color
resonances of ochre shades of amarillo
luminous aching with "la bellezza"
and are there then lordly presences
still among us for whom the quotidian
the vulgar the commonplace ---
nay what is the immense lack in the air
to feel with such immense tenderness
the passage of all things
to break down crying on the sidewalk
beside the narcolept and the pariah
to shake with all the imminence of being
because the mystery has just manifested
wearing the outmoded metaphysick
of 17th century perukes
and we witnesses to the aweful & sublime
thunderstruck on the street corner
designated for the "transbay express"

are simply at a loss to transcribe
and look for some sign in the terse azure
for a burning flag in the cloudwork
to advise us that this *must* be
++++++++++++++++++++++++++
I am haunted by you, Bro
in the lacustrine recesses of the heavens
in the unshaped combs and vales
in the weirs and uncharted rivulets
argent with myth that dapple
the map of the flowering Unconscious
haunted by you haunted by you
up there somewhere above my head
playing your transverse flute
lyrichord monody of the Whole!
when does night ever come
when does night ever come!
haunted by you in the abstract hour
when zenith turns to mercury
when doppelganger marries his shadow
somewhere by the left side of the house
where the sun never shines
and all those little white flowers
pop up like tiny anxious deities
when at last the shepherd returns
placing his crook carefully against stone
waiting to finally transpire
leaving in the grassy maze
the shape of his love the size of ink
to dissolve in the twilight heliotrope
for no one to ever rightly read
haunted by this dissolving
this twilit section of time
that can never be correctly understood
just as you and I were never
correctly understood haunted
by the amazing and distant memory
that spreads like a fog
over the imaginary city you and I built
one day outside of time
++++++++++++++++++++++++++
it's saturday again, Bro

time to open up the poem book
and select a verse or two

Of those that roome was full, and them among
there sate a man of ripe and perfect age
who did them meditate all his life long*

****Faerie Qveene, IX, 54***

11-10-12

(opium the perfume)
nikki arai in memoriam

queen of my heart
how long this devastation
this errant folly of memory
everything's gone wrong
texts fill with bracken water
the days when of a morning
I trudged up green and vallejo streets
always looking for perfection
gone forever despite sky's
azure permanence despite
the imminent fog of life
yours was a regime of hotels
of stolen rooms and boudoirs
of cars that never belonged to you
painted putti fucking in the cornices
airplane tickets to nowhere
finally winding up in anonymity
with your camera eye focused
on the godless who planted tents
on university property
call that a life story
a record of non-events strung
out on the golden chain of being

to define and not define
which was the buddha spirit
and which the infinite daemon
however ancient the arcadia
printed in your vision
it never added up
just a day in the cancer ward
and then night's malignant offal
skewered to the windows
of general hospital waiting
waiting for the invention of spain
to materialize waiting for a miracle
everything turning brown
twilight endless
queen of my heart
the bleeding in hotel durant
was a sign that filled the dark
bodas de sangre!
from the airplane window
all I saw was a teakwood jungle
floating like a wreck
above the ocean of being
from the airplane window
all I felt was that blood drenched
sheet tossed into the tub
why didn't you realize?
there are only so many seconds
in a single day
all the conversations we never had
boil down to a night in chicago
or to all the phone books
I searched looking for a clue
for lady murasaki to manifest
out of the turmoil of alphabets
and relentless speech patterns
why didn't you understand?
the white blood cells
simply ate you up
leaving a skin brown and withered
on the plate glass window
of a chic art gallery in north beach
it couldn't be you there!

queen of my heart
the perfume you wore has spread
like an enormous invisible cloud
all over the world
OPIUM

11-17-12

(beautiful)

it isn't every day
it's today the world ends
it's today clouds crumble
shaking the invisible axles
of the firmament to powder
and on the rim of all juxtapositions
straddling the voice of harmony
the single unit of spain
a guitar jungle-green with energy
breaks down the azure infinite
it's today the world ends
it's today the world really ends
somewhere near the confines of the eye
somewhere that really doesn't matter
sleeping on streets that disappear
into the bay when none are looking
except for you just waking
from the dream of the other life
from the dream of indifferent ratios
where each deity diminishes
in the shadow of your just washed hair
you who have nothing to say
nothing to remind the mirror
that you alone are sustained by
today's world catastrophe
everything rushing invisibly to the vortex
of your indefinable sex

**the immense retrograde of sandstorms
which are the dictionary of the moon
and if you have recourse to language
if you have a notion of memory
that massive languid skein of saliva
inching toward the history of death
intense moments of light
punctuated by the hesitation of ink
you utter nothing winding
in the mercury of your disposal
the intricate arguments of the beautiful
ascending in spherical order
the evolving ruin of the cosmos
it's today the world ends
because you have no clear yesterday
because tomorrow is the redundant cipher
turning your naked spine to zero
phases of water that has no depth
illogical moments outside the known hour
afternoons in the casual dialect
of heat and tsunami
everything rushing invisibly toward breath
toward the winnowing sections of night
when beauty lays down her shadow
your shadow on the bed of superior intellect
things get truncated
windows become absolute
staring into the planetary degradation
which is a spectacular fireworks
conducted inside a hospital
possibly located in the suburbs of reason
madness and incommensurate longing
red shifts becoming nostalgia
elements of grammatical disorder
enormous as the egypt of aphasics
it is not everyday this happens
this penetrating fire in the flesh
this harrowing in the bone
nightmare of the thousand eyelashes
painted black like the lip of uranus
or easily fractured in endless orgasm
it is why I am addressing YOU!**

of all my illusions the bracken weir
the sotto voce of homeric travel
whom I left as I found on the drifting
island of the lotus eaters
migrant blood and philosophic gypsy
dressing and undressing your skin
with all the phantomatic grace
of one who has died so many times
it doesn't matter why
it's today the world ends
it's today the world ends
++++++++++++++++++++++
of one who has died so many times
YOU why I am addressing
today and today only
my beautiful incomprehensible Nenuphar!
in your obsidian pool
reflecting nothing
if not the nothingness up above
as it revolves and revolves
in the fantastic hemisphere
of your illegal memory
echo echo echo
sleeping then in the ear
that records no sound

echo echo echo

11-18-12

(bedlam)

the really pretty one third
from left of the traffic signal
about to put on her medea hair
or simply glaring into the midnight sun
ah yes the focus of our attention

flashing her impossible beauty
for the camera eye
flashing her ineluctable mind
for the postmaster to open
she's the one for any of us
she who just past three AM
had sex with the russian navy
and is ready for the padded walls
to echo her redundant joy
it's not here I wanna be
it's not there I wanna go
all night long a caravan of blinking lights
all night long which way is up
and which way is out
why do you ask
why do you want to know
the three of us in one person
the dove the gate and the pony tail
don't ask them why
their mouths are russet mums
a field of daffodils spreading past
the lonesome hour
I hear the ivy growing in the ear
they hear the ear growing inside the ivy
who can ever say how long it is
how fast it goes within its mobile
and outside the fractured windows
look at the shepherds praying
for christ to descend the heavenly stair
on either wrist the buttonhole of time
extravagant lunacy because the bull
flayed for the event still roars
because the banker with his candle
cannot figure out indigo
such are the clouds of unreason
such the ineffable inks!
it's not here I wanna be
it's not there I wanna go
but the pretty thing third from left
of the broken traffic signal
too impossibly beautiful
too incredibly beautiful

who can want to eat her?
who can desire to consume her?
it's not me it's never in the clouds
severed from color
full of intricate details
about the deity buried in plaster
just outside the *campo santo*
where hovering shades of nameless
exchange minds exchange mouths
whosoever consumeth the flare
whosoever partaketh of the flare
be so damned as to never
we wander amid circular ruins
amid bodies dreaming of saturn
or is it chronos devouring his offspring
she is too beautiful for words
the doctors of hapology deny rumor
spanish sunsets are fixed inside the clock
ringing forever the poem of her skin
granada sevilla alcantara cordoba
we are denied the sea
and whatever shares with the sea its tide
moon rakes applaud the novel's end
foaming at the mouth
biting their lips hands under hands
come go with me to the alcazar
eat me while I am still breathing
dine on me with your powder wigs
shake your box of jewels empty
here is the guadalquivir with its silver fins
come to greet us with a sandstorm
the dastard moor will have his part
combing the recess of her mind
it's not here I wanna be
it's not there I wanna go
she is not the one we thought
when the portals were seized
and the police carried away the iron
too heavy for the waters of lethe
why is she not all together?
why is she not with her bright thought?
hours of second guessing

the vampire next to the refrigerator
minutes dribbled in vain anxiety
I did not ask to be born
nor to presume to die
it's always the other way around
she is not the other one
with the same face in the mirror
we are not the other one
a small god pinned to the lapel
like a microphone
jabbering on about the junction
of the jamuna and the ganges
while section by section the dark
simply disappears

11-21-12

(the long afternoon)

eternity!

green blue distances

moon at four PM
on the rise
like fading aspirin

have we been here before?

absences & longing

recognize nothing

be somewhere else
in the always light

perfection in drifting
c l o u d s

breathe!

depth of the sixth hour
before entering limbo

each hill is a paradise

each tree a symbol
undecipherable

nostalgia for

when the house invisible
separates from time

11-25-12

(sanskrit)

when was the world?
            ***that* long ago?**
was language ever perfect?
fire worship tectonic gods
irreversible the trajectory
from muddy birth to inky death
irregular verb formations
exactly where to put the accent
memorize everything about air
about earth about water
place the sun precisely in the sky
where it can be best pronounced
world but a hazy memory
coming over a narrow mountain path
into this fetid plain punctuated
by water buffalo and boab trees
counting the number of minutes
it takes to become numb with meditation
to return tranced another person

a grammatical monkey blue faced
chanting on distant smoky peaks
what it is about nothingness
lotus and dancing peacock alike
forged in the symmetry of the eye
it seems we are dense as jungles
green with a sybaritic rot
our tongues pierced by a thread
that goes all the way back to heaven
we are nothing if not hands
gesturing in the ritual of darkness
another one and then still another
comes out of the brush naked proclaiming
the total absence of being
the total absence of being
in the sky a sudden flash
and for years an intense indigo rain
washing away the human alluvial
swarming around temple intricacies
wet whorls of moon patterns
that involve the multiple deities of sex
deafened by the immemorial conch
we set into motion sleep
the immense endless night
that gives birth to time
and when we are reborn
when we gather around a table
discussing discussing what is good
what is beautiful what in fact
is the *world*
none there are who can summon to mind
the syntax of the language before birth
the language of the gods
and we remain senseless
attached to a fictive self
following with wary eye the shadow
the dying day casts across the plain
until once again cold and frail
the mind refuses to connect
what was once light
to

11-28-12

(ontology/oncology)

**it all happens in one minute
at the same time that you are "playing"
with girls for the first time
on some autumn field feeling
the mysterious roundnesses beneath
thin layers of clothing and smelling
their breaths faintly scented
anise or peppermint
in the tumult of laughter
everything so enigmatically exciting
you are being cremated**

11-30-12

"smoke stack lightning"
for james balfour

**she's Radha in person
that red hair
those wrap-around shades
that photogenic smile
and she's come to take me
to the Dance
what are bones and shadows
what are makeup cosmetics
shiny buick eights and
tickets to the paris opera
what is anything left in the rain
beggars' compromises**

situations without solutions
what are dreams in comparison
to dancing with Radha
isn't death worth it
isn't death worth
that fling in the sun
that embrace in the dark
when hair and moon and fragrances
of opium and lilac intoxicate
isn't death worth it
that high school cigarette
and spiked coca cola
that furious ignition of the senses
falling off that cliff
into the unembroidered night
ghost riding in a cadillac
headed for a fork in the ganges
until nothing of the self remains
isn't death worth it
sitting side by side with Girlfriend
on the roller coaster to inferno
each as much the other as possible
skin and the passion of skin
to touch forever
obsession and fornication
lunacy incarnate
but the enigma of it all
the what you will
boundless the sea of love
mysterious isn't it
rain torment and thunder clap
"smoke stack lightning"
it's the 9th grade again
spring eternally in bloom
automobile wheels crunch on gravel
amo amas amat
I've got a date with Scheherazade
how can it ever end
when I show up at the door
fifty years have elapsed
what can anything mean
step-father is still there

rifle in hand
in a chrysalis of light
the future hesitates to open
isn't death worth it
epic fragments puzzling
troubadour lyrics
it's the day after time
angel hurtled relentlessly
from infinity's portal
"when cupid shot his dart
he aimed it at my heart"
only to crash into flat-iron
dazed and bewildered
alone on highway one
menaced by human dilemma
threatened by redemption
isn't death worth
that leap off the roof
that loss of consciousness
caused by a single kiss
hugging the beloved
in life's dark ballroom
billie holiday and jo stafford
singing it forever

she's Radha in person
and she's come to take me
to the Dance

12-02-12

(ariadne)

we are all becoming dead
                slowly in-
exorably
beyond the cross walk

and the illusory sand piles
of the pharaohs
"fly the ocean in a silver plane"
which of us monocolor and
soundlessly dreaming the fall
which is silence which
exorably
ignoring the traffic signal
and the labyrinthine passage
of the atreids
slowly and in-
are we caught in the back up
white water rapids
sewage treatment of the
missile crisis in reverse
oblong and obscure scriptures
exorably swinging
from a single thread
hair and its redundancies
packaged in a history of
"see the jungle when it's wet with rain"
with ringlets and silver coils
bright ribbons seraphim
rejoicing on cloud nine
opium and its variants
scattered over the immense skin
of love of love
wet with rain
numb revolving around the moon
like this in-
exorably at the end
each is a book without
reading one blank script
after another in bed with
of choice bundled fur muff
isn't it wonderful this
all becoming dead
language black sea scum
a froth against wild white
water rapids night as
descending us with it takes
with rain of love

wet jungle from a silver plane
to speak with a tom-tom
a battering ram language what
it is blacker now this night
all us becoming dead this
wonderful going around and
exorably   eyes
wet the magic show
each window has taking us
into the vortex here shake
my hand a fly plane silver
round a dizzying her
thread leading us in and out
no more alive than dead
with rain   if could speak
if language this black mess
a labyrinthine   silver rain
a song heard and unheard
every time I take her out
and she fumbles in her purse
and the rimmel runs down
and she wants ever so much
we becoming dead
her with us much as in-
exorably   isn't a mirage
this is living again just
once only and dancing
too   alive over the ocean
dreaming and falling
abandoned
this palace of mists

12-10-12

(elegy)

grains of sand
children
blooms
blood
sunstorm
in the eye

three hundred million firearms
three hundred million firearms
registered in America today
the whole sky cast in gun metal
as earth rounds its lunation
with a crazy misgiving about
the human species and the stores
it houses its values in for profit
abundance of snowflakes and
whirlwinds invisible in the mind
thunderous gestation of new walmarts
wherever they sprout on the land
once sacred to manitou and buffalo
three hundred million firearms
three hundred million firearms
colored like the limitless horizon
of manifest destiny in deep carmine
will the forester green remember
to come home with his winter?
will the seamstress blind in one eye
recall the stitching on planet uranus?
will whoever signed the constitution
with a series of bloody x-rays
step to the podium and address
the nation of hollywood and florida?
how many bullet wounds is eleven
in the body of a single six-year old?
how much can one mother pay
for her credence in the power of rifle?
who is crying in the deer compound?
who is crying in the high school gym?
just how many bullet wounds is eleven
necessary for the body of one seven year-old?
e pluribus unum it says on the brow

of the numinous cloud deity lowering
his purplish stormy mass to the flat ground
is eleven enough bullet wounds
for one six year old flowering in the coppice
hands redolent of proserpina's gore
it takes how much to level the psyche
between sleep and sleep in the drained ear
where an activity of angry bees
where a smithy of enormous darkness
everything gathered in a small brutal fist
a heaven of pink and distance flares
it is afternoon in the archaic stillness
in the remote painting of the last supper
in whatever remains of the face in the mirror
just before dawn before the number
eleven wounds sufficient for a single
six or seven year old and I am crying
with the president and with the sexton
and with the coffin maker
whose face resembles that of betsy ross
the day she entered the mausoleum
in search of the missing thread
three hundred million firearms
three hundred million firearms
somewhere there is an echo
somewhere else the same echo
whispers into infinity

grains of sand
children
blooms
blood
sunstorm
in the eye

(newtown CT)

12-16-12

(new year's eve)

wearing my brother's hands today
morning in an echo of sky cold and infinite
where to place these gnarled hands
these knuckles and joints without feeling
through what dark corridor did he escape
not witnessing this year's foul conclusion
being one with the remotest astral projections
leaving behind his hands for me to puzzle
using them to equate this planet with that
how to play on the traverse flute krishna's song
with these arthritic boney fingers
driving somnolently down ghost avenues
icy white distant endlessly numbered
from one to eternity without order
houses caved in on each other from which
peer ancestors perplexed and german
wrestling with the radio of their memories
to ascertain which brother it is visiting
at such an ungodly hour of predawn
why has no one alerted them to this phantom
to this presence without substance
and suddenly it is past noon in white time
awful resurgence of shadows pleading
for blood and wine at the corner where
memorial parkway reaches into the ether
yet these hands on the driving wheel
pulsating with an other worldly energy
spectral and divine at once sinewy and
whatever else hands have as qualities
as if to write the poem about crematoria
or the advent of the lunar mansion
arrayed with its numinous quarters
all eerily aglow in a distance beyond
comprehension these hands my brother's
pausing in the glass of all reflections
to leave their trace their irregular shape
on the gathering universal dust
and certainly by late afternoon
and it is new year's eve again and
the bottle of gin we shared between us

on a small table in someone's garage
is swiftly consumed passing back
and forth between our identical hands
these hands have transformed themselves
repeatedly through layers of identity
until not only the hands which are my brother's
but the whole section of life known as
the body complex and mysterious
his complex and enigmatic body that is
is quite simply myself originating
in some dark hospital ward deep in winter
where either one of us could be the other
mutually cortical and full of the amazing
unconscious of the human race
kaleidoscopic with kinetic imagery
painting and music and sound of words
passionately disordered creating and
at the same time destroying memory
grass particles wind ovaries silences
between expanding brick and mortar
dancing with a host of minute deities
in a festival of light and blazing
that is breathless and

12-31-12

(chanson)

the intellect doth burn and fly
like smoke into Heaven's eye

did I but heaven forsake and my mind
go wandering lost to itself and old
what spheres bright and fiery then
would bring their splendid light
to this wearisome trek up life's steep
and rugged defiles through what
morasses profound as sleep's utter

gloom and spent spinning a guttered
smoke my soul what book would it read
what small signs espy in that vast
empyrean what anything of balm
to a stranger in a foreign continent
is there but the ennui of distant sand
or the immense and ceaseless roaring
of the salty wave against the shoals
+++++++++++++++++++++++++++++++
thus dreamed the penitent on his rock
a hand did plunge into the smoking air
++++++++++++++++++++++++++++++++
who spoke into the unframed ear?
who announced with ancient sound
the enormous trajectory of the stars?
++++++++++++++++++++++++++++++++
witless in the strife of light and breath
the shepherd a thousand miles from home
nowhere   his flocks
++++++++++++++++++++++++++++++++++
when I told mother I was returning
and it was a dead of winter hoary frost
no shelter from the biting northern blast
I was wounded and knew not why
and there were burning clouds with
flowers of amazing stripe   red
++++++++++++++++++++++++++++++++++
shifts   a loaded deck of cards
on the table next to the   knife
looked warily   her apron
could no longer embrace me as of yore
spun   a   fable
+++++++++++++++++++++++++++++++++
an engine it seemed did check the speed
yet as never before the planet
through the immense night did
                         fissures rent wide
a fire   as large as the Hour
how did we think to go back
                 islands   caves
+++++++++++++++++++++++++++++++++
errant grasses mallows reeds storm bent
a sudden rush of water through stone

memory
++++++++++++++++++++++++++++++++
yet persistence against tempests
did howl and blind messengers
coveted the daughter her white
like berries her to bring forth
by dawn who are then these
+++++++++++++++++++++++++++++++
savage by turns and the music as if drawn
from the leaves of trees voices
bleeding
+++++++++++++++++++++++++++++++
a moth in love with the flame
spelled one by one the words
if one could understand
if one could only comprehend what
went before on knees
bruised would mother recognize
+++++++++++++++++++++++++++++++
enormous sculpted works as if airborne
far above the flute's faint song
men like you and I struggling
+++++++++++++++++++++++++++++++++
molt eron douç mei consir

01-06-13

ALONE

"nous séparer était, en quelque sorte,
nous anéantir"
j.-j. rousseau

across what steppes what prairies what deserts
don't you hear the lonesome train whistle
your flitting wayward soul in its vast winter
intransigent luminous distant
what's to commemorate? what's to celebrate?

I am driving this vehicle charged
with two tons of pure energy
right into the bay and on the radio it says
***"you belong to me"* what can never be**
again and enormous clouds roll into view
and the mass of tectonic plates which is earth
seems to sway and dance for a brief minute
name as many gods as you want
be whatever reincarnation of the buddha you want
"fly the ocean in a silver plane"
this is not charades at some innocent gathering
this is not an object of curiosity in a northern cave
nor a drunken soiree at the Valencia ballroom
this is being alone somewhere in the ionosphere
alone somewhere beyond the last golf links
where suddenly dark absorbs the landscape
alone when only the echoes of houses like glass
resound faintly in the dead sleeper's ear
wasn't there supposed to be a great flame
an immense conflagration just inches above
the terrestrial surface?   dumb
memory of your shadow sits frozen in the car
if there were a purpose to this breathing
to this frosting up the january window
to this being alone side by side with an imaginary urn
yes somewhere in the hospital's vast labyrinth
the place of unrecorded remembrances
watching as through an aquarium
the enormous silent figures of the fathers
glide treacherously near yet oblivious
of any living presence
and I am steering this vehicle
on and through the planetary orbit
to some unknown destination
to some point in the farthest reaches of space
where language has no hold
and everything we have ever thought
is a matter of open dissolution and dust
the enervating endlessness of alone
"maybe you'll be lonesome too
                    and blue"
it can never come back

white turns to blank
shifts in the current
eddying waters
no foot steps
twice

01-21-13

VISHNU

snakes elephants tortoises gnats
temple ruins jungle froth red glow
stone cut from air stone cut from nothing
immense skies swirling in a vedic strophe
mud spit sperm rishis' divine curses
to breathe for a minute only open space
millions of astral bodies condensed
to a black spot beneath the eyelid
to be born tangential yellow whirling
clouds thunder rain hailstones blisters
lightning in the form of a maiden
copulating for ages on a mountain peak
to be born again stench of blood
stained skin parchments illegible
hundreds of languages stuttering tongues
correct pronunciation phonetic decay
snakes elephants tortoises gnats
cities swarming with black and red ants
labyrinth of time in circular epochs
holy wars arisen from human error
body parts scattered to the winds
countless times the same accident recurs
sleep dark endless swoon and childhood
passing in the blink of an eye unrecorded
whole transformations of chemistry
eddying pools of water encircling eternity
how is it we are found here in this consciousness

looking for spears of green grass and air
dispatches from the gods irregular verbs
and to be born again inside a round temple
cow's milk ghee curds oaten reeds whistles
everyone who has passed though here will die
explosion follows explosion monuments of dust
history's miserable undecipherable script
hollow efficacy of science warring lunacy
snakes elephants tortoises gnats
born again stuck in a loop fission
attrition depression aggression holocaust
mind altering drugs sex speed light
innocence songs moonbeams nothing lasts
transposed heads nuclear immediacy
passing through walls of smoke divinities
angels excoriated by visions of the end
"filling empty houses without paying"
avatars enormous and formless walking
here amongst us minds like horizons
who can know this without going crazy
when was the last time you went to the state hospital
when was the last time you went downtown
to shop for an orthopedic device
angels excoriated by visions of the end
and still keep being reborn stimulated
by philosophies from the far east
marching through forests of dead legions
always in search of always in search of
mansion with precisely twenty eight chambers
twelve avatars of Vishnu anthropomorphic
dancing on the seed of annihilation
massive distances where everything happens
without memory
complex linguistic structures porous rock
hegemonies of beryl sapphire emerald jasper
ennui sans souci performance enhancing drugs
diapason of all terrestrial thrills
sand dung muck ire & envy
of all that is bright and shining youth
that once lived on perpetual lawns
maggots children with devil faces
catastrophes beyond count conflagrations

sun storms lunar eclipses planetary deviation
when was the last time you visited her home
when did you ever contrive it was love
names of female deities come to mind
ovarian cancer "bodas de sangre"
snakes elephants tortoises gnats
shadowy figures driving great vehicles
in the back yard of a summer night
constellations palaces of constant fire
blazing texts where it is written "come no more"
exhaustion age declining strength death
yet to be reborn amid flocks of sheep
dwelling in arcadian dales wearing masks
arrived but never reaching the Gate
this is hell this is instant hell this is
automobile graveyard and gothic cathedral
hell in the instamatic camera that develops
images of the indwelling god
ghouls vampires succubi lovelorn girls
"I am orestes!" a voice from torn leaves
the trek to the orient of symbology
mandarins 5000 years old dozing on cataclysm
a buddha takes place in the system of avatars
shopping carts full of ancient bodies
imagination   the mind
writing and rewriting endless hymns
paeans to the nameless immortals
whose very absence is a kind of ignition
alcoholism dereliction nymphomania
narcissism and necrophilia virtues all
humankind a pageant of missing persons
poetry at last in place of rational thought
stark naked goddesses eating mortal flesh
rabid encounters with the "other"
exactly where nothing matters
silence before the final Big Bang
silence that is sleeping forever
a tiny dream in marble
spikes of fluid light transforming
things that come in go in dark basements
hands exchange hands
prayer wheels ablaze

vast organizations of night
what will come of this creation
what will disappear from view
behind glass the twin brother beckoning
to the Vishnu avatar in eternal descent
how is it we are found here in this consciousness
looking for spears of green grass and air
SNAKES ELEPHANTS TORTOISES GNATS

01-26-13

(the light bearer)

I was on my way to Jerusalem one bright morn
shimmering glass its towers round I espied
suddenly in raiment dazzling white I myself found
not one I was accustomed to be but Other
bearing in my right hand a lit flare and in my left
the nothing of all compounded air condensed
a vision this is a distance of many times magnified
not myself the other I am to be this cancelled now
this morn so bright a moon at once behind
my shoulder bloomed and waned so fast I deem
I scarce any other thing could notice asleep I was
on what unknown road to what absent place
what drug was coursing through my veins
what memory made my heart palpitate so
in how many realms simultaneously adrift
from peak to peak I launched a flaming sphere
and far below the midden heap of earth did glow
how was I myself to know if now an other am
what suchness of night what cloudwrought zeal
what manyness all around the atmosphere burned
such is me I woe this strangest dream of time
if there was me somewhere else if there was other
swirling entities so many times dead and bound
in a swoon of state I am rapt a music ancient rings

between each ear a hundred summers green resound
an anvil in place of winter a sweet syringe in spring
and from lawns eternal swarm faces of young girls
each who me takes in deep embrace and darkness
swells the brain and reels the mind in muddy torrents
until in some else wise remoteness fast in outer space
I wake fixed in glassy rounds of shimmering towers
the Jerusalem I sought in me rewinds its Hour
the Jerusalem in me I sleep in its forever brow
and I am Joe once again beside the silent water
and I am Joe   once again

01-27-13

(legend)

to live in mythical times
to cast spears of light into the galactic sea
to be at one with the enduring seed-flame
to live in mythical times
to remain innocent between tree and rock
awaiting the perennial king
the one whose mask you also wear
the twin in time of the other self
to live in mythical times
chasing through field and meadow
the shadow shortened by noon
escorted by echo and her dazzling maids
invisible in swart ivy clinging
to drink to the dregs the heady white drug
to see once and only once what is beyond
and to remember with the ear
the liquid song of water in cool rills
to be at the beginning
to be at the beginning of things
wild wind darkness distances unlit
to begin naming things

osprey nutmeg sunflower widow
to offer to the night unholy dreams
something warm and viscous
gliding down her inner thigh
to be at once in the beginning of things
and inert the root of a tree a stone
watching from a remoteness light gathering
over the dumb mountain peak
spreading again gracefully into the plain
naming things as they appear and are used
hand hatchet hair lips and surf
standing at the beginning where shore
yields its sandy being to the brine
to live in mythical times
in orchards or grottos
clinging to shadowy presences
even in their mysterious absence
weeping uncontrollably for no known reason
or because at sunset things begin to disappear
who you are is of little count
clouds as immense as continents anger the heavens
thunder peals roll endlessly through the Hour
in mythical times a surfeit of red
thick hair unkempt of one who is already a deity
shimmering in wet skin the goddess
who takes from the crops and herds
what she never returns
to cast spears of light into the galactic sea
prayers unanswered but for the small rain
that punctuates the great Year unexpectedly
in myth trying to remember who That was
harp anvil gorse bosom sleep
naming things unfound but in depths
of memory white green and yellow reefs
lifted like feathers into the dense sky
pyramids of carved rock pivoted like shafts
into the music of air and trembling
as if in an after life of thought
mind so at once everywhere then extinguished
by a flint-tipped missile or a jealous fist
naming things in the long meandering
between a remembrance of tangled wetness

and the huge mound erected to recall
the husk of bones buried below
who was a king divining a future in leaves
now a dry soot that stains the shivering ether
coming round in circles ever wider
to live in mythical times
to be at one with the enduring seed-flame
curled up by the cliff side
when summer gradually erodes into autumn
passing mouths around the crackling fire
to elicit elegiac sounds of mourning
trying to understand the enigma
carving on hard surfaces odd symbols
to make of them a meaning
a sense of the going away
passing from a life
into the mystery
mythical

02-15-13

"variations on a stanza by Vidyapati"

"the deer, the moon, the lotus and gold,
the cuckoo and elephant – all six-fold
can be seen in her eye, face, fragrance, grace,
in her sweet speech and elegant pace"

deer moon lotus gold , the the the and
this crazy space this jungle place all
her eye face fragrance grace all fold
cuckoo and elephant in her elegant pace
and sweet speech what of hers morn
and night like gold poured into the lotus
no one can hear what dark lisping
sound like water coming to its end
sleeping drowned in that fragrance

grace her elegant elephant pace
a cuckoo her voice this all six-fold
who can her name a place between and
be seen yet in her eye its gold and lotus
moon and deer feeding on her breasts
shadows adrift the distance beyond "the"
and each symbol grace and fold six
her eye embrace deer and moon still
in the evening's drifting hour of ink
a drowsy jungle place this crazy space
her fragrance do embrace gold the lotus
born in elegance her pace like elephant's
on waters dark and deeper still the night
's inky space her gold and deer the moon
apace mirage jewel encrusted cuckoo
her face in space her fragrance and grace
shivering shadows in water moon embrace
maddened hips shifting in lotus memory
her grace six-fold in her eye no trace
her sweet speech a distance darkening
cuckoo a bed a deer a grass a plain beyond
"the" and where deer and hind and roe
small arrows flee that love does fling
moon rings gold elephant pace her elegance
grace the endless night six-fold her
jungle place her bed a lotus a grace
this cup do hold a lip does taste fragrance
to behold her elephant and cuckoo
dusky voice singing in evening's velvet
pace her grace a deer a moon and lotus
gold painted shimmering on a single leaf
repeat her and the and the no sound
require as lapse in time her eye embrace
a pace silent and chaste no foot regards
nor touches earth nor raises dust
above her eye and grace sweet speech
her face the deer the moon the lotus
and gold her elegance and eye
her grace

02-17-13

DE PROFUNDIS

**the face you were talking to in the mirror
not your face the absence of a face talking
who was it said about skin that every seven years
and down at the shore gilded ships sails unfurled
ghosts voices calling through ropes and hawsers
technically dead the child in you resumes
what you were saying to the inert glass
to the image on the other side was darkness
clouds above rolling in deep orange purple
talking to someone else the other afternoon
about the chasm between us the abyss
using a plural noun formation to imply
sadness at the core the bottoms of water
what little sun there was eked through cracks
to let in a small light you said wasn't there
an engine somewhere inside the body knows
when to shut off when to drown the soul
music of the moment with punctuated rhythms
what cargo the boats carried silk in abundance
fragrances wafted from the cliffs of sea
into these unlit quarters where waking
you are not assured this is a new day**
        "flores para los muertos"
**like fruit ready to rot soft unpleasant to touch
you said was not sufficient to explain the soul
's demise the oriental tragedy the eumenides
in the glass something like mercury shifting
everything caught off balance a face blank
emerging from the chaos of so many absences
how many such hours indwelling you suffer
cease counting and watch the storm gathering
above the shivering masts of mid morning
can you recall exactly what was slithering
along the wall just before dawn the poem**

**an ancient fragment with rock and alabaster
about beauty or a lip against the cup
daffodils smothering the egress
a body suddenly lifted to heaven glowing
brilliantly like another sun beyond human ken
from the old shape left listless on earth
shattered everything like interrupted dreams
looking in the grass for the shadow that once
lay there praying for the sky god to descend
and did it ever happen did the voice beckon
in an alley children shouting into evening's muffled
going to bed later on in life still hearing them
shouting a word game nonsense softly
night apprehensive shuts the door**

02-21-13

PALINURUS

nudus in ignota, Palinure, iacebis harena
Aen. V, 871

**immense the loss
                    islands
where cytherea danced on the skiff of time
who will   ponder this
elegance   gods dressed in distance
do sleeping now in cloudy raiment
          go into their absence
no more cleave to rock   nor diamond
shattered   loss suffer
promontories lifted into the burning
   aether   shifted from red
next to uranus the mount seraphic shines
and down below do we mortals shudder
dreaming   is it another life
other than the one we assume is
       colors from a planet gone amiss
suddenly graduating from high school**

pomp and circumstance dizzy
mist before the eyes   felled
certainly   some one else knocking
night   umbratile images wavering
a long distance call
someone's son is dead
did not see rightly the future
like an oncoming vehicle alcoholic
theogony   felt this immense loss
this aching no void could fill and wept
when the police officer
islands astray
drifting without godhead   lives
sea mists cliffs remote peaks heat urgency
but palinurus is drowned seeking
what errant star   amiss
cytherea danced
air never seemed lighter
burning burning
beneath the olympian bed beneath
somewhere else   is asking
to become someone else   water
by itself shifted from Okeanos
to some far flung asteroid where
immense this sense of loss adrift   boundlessly

am I still the one I thought
islands cut off from
delving deeper into the brine
a single finger evolving
like language
in its most archaic form   shapes
moving through memory of grass
listening in the tepid afternoon
to the single invisible airplane overhead
and below diving senselessly
into the watery element
through memory of ivy
rushing to accept the dark

02-22-13

"sundays"

for james balfour, again

**driving around late sunday afternoons
winter in the countryside snow disheveled
hills and black naked tree limbs gesticulating
toward the moribund orange disc of sun
descending into its daily avernus somewhere
behind the sprawling mayo estate with its
small deer quivering in the empty paddock
who we were being sick with ennui and
not wanting to go home to be anywhere
but here in this chill planetary horizon**
every moment has its own mythology
**there are constellations and galaxies
so sublime one shivers at the thought
about to enter the darkest quadrant
such luminous entities once bore a name
huddled in a vehicle ourselves searching
a mind to cling a thought to some ivy
ever green in this bleakest season
late sunday afternoons as if drugged
circling the same every time around
long country roads snow ditched
on either side curving off into nowhere
wind soughing through scattered pines
so lonesome only the radio for company
etching in the oncoming dark a lyric
that promises a distance of almost tropical
beauty so rare against the frosted pane
not wanting to go home even as sun
drops its last orange violet reflection
upon the endless blackening horizon**
every moment has its own mythology
**no windows where to see lighting
what is distance when life is ennui
where to go after the last bend in the road
not wanting the sense in the pit of the gut
a horizon without seams blends into
constellations and galaxies so sublime
turning to the other in search of a name
could it be he is there no more a face**

gone into the blackened glass released
and howling in the deep ravines snow
ditched entrance to avernus where sun
its last rays lays gently down to die
what is the gift of life the seed immense
but to bear death in each quickened breath
outside see there is no one calling
no small deer left in the empty paddock
a radio sending messages into night
songs driven by static into uncoded
signals of pyramids and market place
descend with some small latin into hell
every sunday all sundays this eternal
circling dense hills unlit presences almost
holy the touch is gone scanners from afar
indian ghosts assembling a different sky
from the one learned in sunday school
immense beings like gods invisible
falling out of the last place to go
manitou and buffalo spirits drunk
raving into sleep some dark alcoholic tale
every moment has its own mythology
again music of remoteness switching
dark snow pitched dells small deer sniffing
frozen grass the face in the pond below ice
as if beckoning the hundred and one lessons
of grammar to resume the engine of syntax
derelict resemblances mounds of dirt
something inert breathless sick with ennui
driving around sunday afternoons late
to make of that *the* moment of life
reference sublime before going forth
into the dazzling otherness that follows

02-25-13

"last ode for claire birnbaum"

Goin' to Chicago
Sorry but I can't take you

i

**looking for traces of claire birnbaum
in the suburbs of chicago today
superhuman entities hovering over
wheaton bible college where
red-demon-eyed baptist ministers
denounce adherents of the torah
in the "loop" frank sinatra's voice
drowns out the wabash avenue "el"
everything is out of funk
a sort of jazz
syncopated rhythms
from lake michigan
where fish surface belly up mysteriously
dead as are we all
technically speaking
scenario recall heat and inebriation
iron mill grist smoking high indiana
where dirty skunk river empties
into myth of ojibway and cherokee
and you and me, joe
in the B&K theater
watching charlton heston part the red sea
disgusted we walk into humidity
drenched atmosphere at once alert
to the invention of memory and
all the drum beats that destroy it
who can never return
is the question
marriage to the first of twenty brides
in the month of zinc teethwork
heard that before?
55th street
staring at the demolition that used
to be the old Beehive where Bird
used to play
or so they say**

grass destroyed by the cyclotrons
that hum with a manic Platonism
I don't get it, joe
the bookstore where we dawdled
thumbing through marxist tractates
get with it, joe
the guy burning the american flag
upside down is a black pacifist
got my mojo working
coming home on a heat drenched
afternoon claire pulls off her clothes
sitting in her maidenform bra
in a living room empty of air
but for whitney's sanskrit grammar
paint spackled conjugations
vedic breathings
where's the error, joe?
claire preparing a Seder
for the first time away from home
lots of wine and breaking matza
the stranger was me
big table ritually spread
but you weren't there, joe
the way things go
way things went astray
missed the boat
fell off the wagon
massive binges on 63rd street
pawning your face for a few bucks
got my mojo working
woodlawn avenue stretching for miles
anonymous structures ready to burn
cut your wrists on glass
suddenly winter night
breath sticks in the air
white plumes of life frozen
or waking on rooftop
above jimmy's bar
ashtray for a mind shouting
for the dawn goddess to come down
goes on forever
massive quadrants of utopian city

stretching into the prairie
claire pulling out
said she'd be back in a few weeks
never returned
holocaust survivor
diaphragm missing from the cabinet
movie theaters vagrant
tombs sifting through mercury
latin hexameters memorized scansion
but it just won't work on you
who invented memory?
nymph echo narcissus hyacinth
dive into pool of senselessness
hospital on ellis avenue
not sure of the street names
blend of epic and personal
long afternoons in the bar
quaffing something dark
like the lethe
summer in all the windows forever
joe, forever
that dense green foreboding
but it just won't work on you

ii

everything becomes myth
the long night trip over Appalachia
to underwood street NE
in the nation's capitol pressed under
a sky at once spring-like and immortal
doomed sequences out of synch
with memory the evasive underlying
isn't it just like death to go on like this
frank sinatra's voice echoing in the lobby
of carrara marble and antiphonies of doo-wop
mud becomes cloud cloud turns to dust
rain just over the horizon and sounds
of war drumming in the sleeping ear
woodlawn avenue flat endlessly silent
after the last exam and Hannibal
has just crossed the alps and Livy is

writing it all down in jazz strophes
practiced dormitories of strangled ivy
dancing in their sleep nubile things
who have just come back from spring break
and now june is hot and tempestuous
with its unstrung pianos and unsure
future in newspaper wrappers turning
brown like the walls intense with nostalgia
who will be hitchhiking instead of
looking for a job near the Wrigley building
in love to break out of jungles drunk
imitating the breath that inspired Hesiod
is no longer wearing the same face
is on a highway becoming a poet
once if I could remember, joe
mutations   verse

02-27-13

(lachrimae rerum)

it's deeper than that
much more   silent
a rift in time   air
and darker too   space
memory's   tomb
wing white flut-   earth
reflections   eye
and much farther   child
tering quietly   dust
legend of heaven   water
cling to nothing   empty
saffron robes   breath
deeper still   grief
stepping stones   float
sorrowing bird   song
broken gate   weeds

beyond the root tears
letting hands go ear
is ending soon pain
love's brief heart
what's over now soul
release me lips
deny being shhh
red shifts
elements on fire
in all ten directions
moon stone falling
shadow figures smoking
their lives away
who among us them
code-switching dialects
makes no sense
a blade of grass separates us
pornography
when last seen she was
wearing nothing but rain
if I am lucid
by fits and starts blue
a hallucination in the arm
chakras spine
radha without krishna
when the pleiades pour
their liquid light
and
all earth in its abundance
fails
green shoots tender
shores of the bosporus
letters written home
mom dead
was it last tuesday we buried
her?
immense with grief
faltering
under the weight of saturn
who ate his children
can we ever straightened
become detached

to nothing
at each new turn envelopes
gold dust iniquity
foil crickets
shield of achilles mandala
loam damp
a articles
kept bawling like a child
sat there in the dirt
hands sifting
seas
of pain unless
dark
after waiting for several hours we became alert
with dread waiting for them to come home,
waiting for the reassuring sound of the car
wheels crunching on the gravel, waiting for
them to come home hoping they were not some
how dead in a ditch their necks broken blood
drilling out of their ears, for the crunch of
car wheels on the gravel of the driveway, and
it was always so late we never slept until that
sound of gravel crunching, the car doors opening
and slamming shut, their voices drifting
as if in a dream, or drunk, alive

03-01-13

(the girlfriend)

how many times do I have to tell you
leave me alone!
all this swirl of avatars and non-avatars
and worlds and hells and salvations
and destructions rishis and mendicants
going solo into the woods and deities
a millionfold coming and going bright

and dark shining and not shining crossing
the sea-of-being or drowning in water
the size of a cow's hoof how can it know
and be known who can say this is that
and not the other in this maze of galaxies
asterism planets dark-stars day dreams
and eventualities can this be consciousness
light and being sleep and waking walking
in this time and not the other time the past
not the present who can say this is future
already in a maze of museums and galleries
where everything is collected and labeled
don't touch it says everywhere the body
not the soul the virgin not the queen
changing sex in the middle of the day
becoming the girlfriend crying in her locker
because it will not come to pass love
the dance on saturday night the pigeons
cooing abracadabra in the dawn hours
when the troubadours drunk on nostalgia
create and pine after her drifting in her
prom dress night after night star shine
brightest heavens one after another song
devotion utterly infatuation obsessed with
the dark lord strutting in his blue skin
on the other bank of the stream playing
his bamboo flute driving all the girls crazy
about salvation and trance and migration
of souls one after the other destined to
be born 84,000 times before becoming
perfect as is girlfriend today crying in
her locker staring into broken mirror
the how many faces in those bits of glass
all her all her striving for otherness for
the unit of time beyond time to be no more
red shifts dwarf stars blue shifts black
holes big bangs lunacy waking in a different
bed wearing someone else's clothes
talking all night long to the wall where
hanging the big picture behind glass glows
maddened and clear headed at once
knowing when to dance when to go barefoot

when to tear all her clothes off when
to dive into the Yamuna when to resurface
being dead and alive being totally dead
shaking water off her body turning
the soul inside out on the grass to dry
singing with a different voice high sweet
but with incomprehensible words
hobson jobson creole pidgin hill dialect
while black bee buzzing flies in and out
of the melody swarming honey in the air
above her head above her thoughts above
the world which never was above grass
and dirt and ant-heaps and mulch
this is the world this is the tenuous reality
this is nowhere this is the imagination
working with its crepuscular flares
to illumine for a moment only the girlfriend
to isolate her to single her out to betray
+++++++++++++++++++++++++++++++
which one is yours?
I don’t really remember
a small moon pasted to her brow
maybe or with a corsage of paper poppies
blushing waiting just waiting
to dance
again

03-04-13

(heaven, or, the postcard
from Thailand)

look into Desire!
fire burning higher
light me up shadow
dream me up flame
don’t touch there

don't smoke there
move as shadows
burn as flame
moth drawn forever
into Desire's eye

shapes of smoke
clouds wayward
wisps floating away
Desire's thin flame
charged dreamlike
into the mass of hair
lighting it up like day
in eternal noon
red ebullience
of music cataracts
turning afterthoughts
into railroad trestles
over which wheels
of steam hiss
violently erotic
in heaven that is
in heaven where
forever moth burns
in passion's heat

I have known women
who could not keep
their eyes off me
& I have seen crystal
stairway ascending
poets do not know
I have received
from Thailand
the postcard where
Vishnu shakes
too hot to handle
the goddess wily
in wild Thailand
green snakes that
slither across sands
gibbons in the jungle

hooting and humid
hair wet with sweat
pelting warm rain
offerings of roseapple
and dragonfruit
left at Spirit house
is that not heaven?

doorways entranced
teakwood steaming
rice bowls green
papaya and garlic
someone's eyes
attached to me
emerging from one
earth going into
another earth
distant as Desire

03-12-13

(ensimismado)

lost in thought
where water meets sky
white wings cloud surf
lost summer hours memories
days green as wanton grasses
shape of bodies in dreams
falling and falling forever
from depths of immobile space
to the earth beneath earth
proserpina's garden legend
heat crystallized in mind
shifts red stellar oceans
myth of atomic creation
nihil ex nilo gigni potest

lost in thought
forever falling dream
of bodies shaped like ink
where water emerges from sky
and sky's immobile flame
envelopes all time since birth
summer hours lost memories
greener than wanton grasses
days of archaic horizons
distances underworld legend
crimson embroidery inside the eye
watching rapt universe disappear
& reappear in a grain of sand
heat become dense as crystal
mind the mirror of its double
twins returning to zero
mother the ineffable goddess
span of quartz in myth
hand invisible forming night
before everything pales at dawn
rooftops flying away into mountains
deities tumbling inside a music
of raucous perpetuity
smoke shadows smoke
then silence
ensimismado
cliffs of origination remote
waterfalls of imagined nations
dust in quantities beyond scope
translations of pure air
into ether the gassy ramparts
fire transduced into seismic vowels
flashing rages of an anterior heaven
burning burning eternally
memories grassy wanton shapes
body against body in heat
crystallized ruins of the archaic
cities thin as mint-leaf built
one upon the other
mind a hazy dream
thirsting for
silence

03-12-13

(summers come and go)

the way things move
dark passages
like the swooping swallows
at the cliff of Gubbio
before sunset
universal transept
caught between air and air
a single thin flame
mortal breath
could you have been
so close trembling
in the wild outback
taken suddenly
by some black rust
working its way
into unsuspecting entrail
was it the sky’s other face
network of lightning
and cricket song
drilled a path
into your diverted mind
keen winds honing
invisible dovecotes
where hidden small
deities map their universe
small stores of mint
sage and parchment
statues on the moon
turned blind by a code
you were sure
was known to you alone
brief storms in history
which you kept erasing
with the talisman
of your strange fictions
the way things move
no more through any month

summers come and go
painted fans held
by women whose hips
your hands grazed
in museums of ruin
tiny grass plots
dedicated to the unnamed
through yellow hours
a hundred sighs
sleeves empty of arms
a children's playground
somewhere in the beyond
this wreck of smoke
this engine derailed
hollyhocks and patience
beside the gravel drive
you murmur in a shell
to seas of unknown space
bright reds billowing
like inks of thought
submerged forever
in the distant azure
where nothing is heard
and no echo returns

03-13-13

CODA

(sleep-walking)

I'll be looking at the moon
But I'll be seeing you

by virtue of your shadow
you have passed the corpse-eaters
and come to the Divine Doors
restless for the breath you lack

**you come and lie down beside me
to entertain the perhaps of an idea
the retrograde motion of sleep
in disguise azure and transparent
almost as if water didn't matter
nor the many petty deities lurking
in the just mown grass there
where you almost lost a finger
I can't stop you from wandering
you get up from the bed no sooner
did you lie down hands folded
eyes forever shut a sack of ashes
with memory and yearning for
no I can't stop you from just going
into the ether scattering thoughts
like sand into the fourth dimension
shaking the titles off the books
you kept hidden from the librarian
what did you leave me? your voice?
just as I was asleep last night I heard
you whisper something delicate
into my ear and I started up looking
but you were already past the Lintel
opening what appeared to be the gold
and massy Divine Doors however shadowy
however remote intangible illusory
was it a phone book in your left hand
or the great map of los angeles in 1945?
if we go back to playa del rey school
to dance around the big sombrero
who will tell which of us is the first
which of us the last to understand
that there is no identity only its replica
and yet you keep sleep-walking
coming down the celestial stair
to rest in grand-dad's leather rocker
dust and shadows of dust all eternity
what is it that I cannot see?
what is it that I cannot hear?
immemorial as ever the "other"
embarking   seas of intellect
become seas of dust   shadows**

what was a brother
a window an apse a tower a vault
history of rust an accident in alcohol
peering through a lens opaque
to the opposite bank of the river Lethe
where gather small white flowers
the disembodied hands of the fathers
weeping obdurate on their spears
it was a vision, joe
just a vision being here on earth
meandering the meadows bright
one summer morn
from afar the sun
glinting reflecting on the Divine Doors
where now you go sleep-walking
grass stained image breathless
shadowless

03-22-13

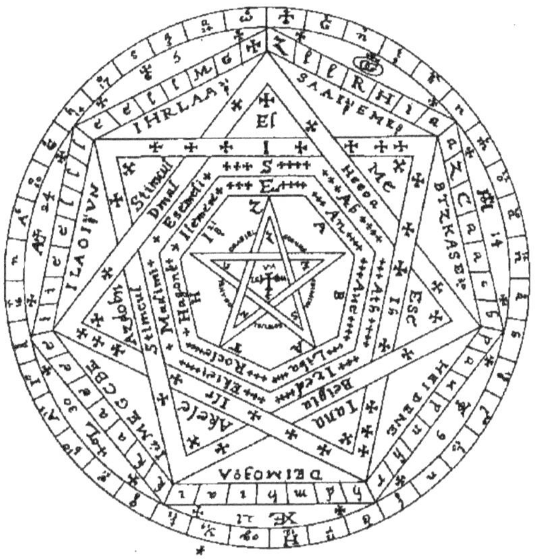

Ivan Argüelles is an American innovative poet whose work moves from early Beat and surrealist-influenced forms to later epic-length poems. He received the Poetry Society of America's William Carlos Williams Award in 1989 as well as the Before Columbus Foundation's American Book Award in 2010. He is the twin brother of renowned New Age writer, José Argüelles. As a young poet in the late fifties and early sixties, Argüelles felt the influence of the Beats but also immersed himself in the literature of Romance languages and High Modernism. Upon graduation from Vanderbilt, Argüelles was hired as a cataloger at the New York Public Library. It was there, in the library's poetry collection, that he discovered the poets of the New York School. As he later wrote in an autobiographical essay, "Asi Es la Vida," "What was this idiom, this racy colloquial and yet often surreal mélange? I was still swinging with Dante and the troubadours . . .And then there was the gateway to the French surrealists through Ashbery and O'Hara . . .My mind was in flames, multiplying in all directions. . . Between Vallejo and Breton my brain began to sunflower." But the turning point came with his discovery of the poetry of Philip Lamantia. As Argüelles stated, "Lamantia's mad, Beat-tinged American idiom surrealism had a very strong impact on me. Both intellectual and uninhibited, this was the dose for me." While Argüelles's early writings were rooted in neo-Beat bohemianism, surrealism, and Chicano culture, in the nineties he developed longer, epic-length forms and eventually returned, after the first decade of the new millennium, to shorter, often elegiac works exemplary of romantic modernism. His many books include: *Instamatic Reconditioning* (1978), *The Invention of Spain* (1978), *Captive of the Vision of Paradise* (1982), *Tattooed Heart of the Drunken Sailor* (1983), *Manicomio* (1984), *What Are They Doing to My Animal?* (1984), *Nailed to the Coffin of Life* (1986), *The Structure of Hell* (1986), *Pieces of the Bone Text Still There* (1987), *Baudelaire's Brain* (1988), *Looking for Mary Lou: Illegal Syntax* (1989), *"That" Goddess* (1992), *Hapax Legomenon* (1993), *Tragedy of Momus* published in the anthology *Terminal Velocities* (1993), *Enigma & Variations* (1995), *Purisima Sex Addict II,* with Jake Berry (1997), *Dead/Requiem,* with Jack Foley (1998), *Saint James*, with Jack Foley (1998), *Madonna, a Poem* (1998), *Daya Karo* (1999), *City of Angels* (1999), *Madonna Septet* (2000), *Cosmic Karma Raga,* with Peter Ganick (2000), *Chac*

***Prostibulario,* with John M. Bennett (2001), *Tri Loka* (2001), *Orientalia* (2003), *Inferno* (2005), *Comedy, Divine, The* (2009), *The Death of Stalin: Selected Early Poems* (2010), *Ulterior Vision(s)* (2011), *A Day in the Sun* (2012), and *The Second Book* (2012).**

Testimonials

If anyone is capable of generating an *ars poetica* in this or any other century it is Ivan Argüelles. For decades he has composed poetry every day by the boundless luminescence of intuition, informed by deep and extensive erudition in several languages, and by the sheer muscle of heart at the nexus of brain. No other contemporary poet brings such passion and intelligence to the art or sings with such vivid experimental lyricism. We have waited for, and requested, a new collection of poems from Argüelles. Here it is at last—a selection from infinity. Drink deep and long. Expect transformation.

—Jake Berry

Ivan Argüelles shows, in this selection of recent work, that he is one of the most visionary poets of our time. His grand themes are Death and the Eternal Feminine, and their mutual implication; with a poetic power and range reminiscent of Pound's *Cantos*, Argüelles integrates Eastern and Western mythology with pop-culture icons to call down his muse. Argüelles's language seems charged with superhuman energies; his cadences are nothing less than driving, desperate, and dizzying, coming ever closer to attaining an unattainable union with the divine. Ivan Argüelles is that rarest of poets: one who practices at the very precipice of being.

—Andrew Joron

When a reader encounters the poetry of Ivan Argüelles, it is not unlike entering the workroom of a latter-day alchemist who delves deeply into the lyrical limits of the English language, and beyond. Argüelles possesses a shamanic soul that is heart-rending in its expansiveness and its bold journey toward celebrating our intuitive possibilities in the realm of literature. For Argüelles, poetry is a field for endless invention, and, in *Ars Poetica*, invent he does. It is a collection monumental in scope, a true sourcebook for our era.

—Neeli Cherkovski

Against the End

doesn't end the cr
own mid.dle point a
gainst the d.u.s.t.y syn
tax in ches wh irring "in
the grass" 's other temp
le ag *ainst the w i n d*
it's ear c rashing "at th
e en trance" ,bric-a-brac in
the shallow grave *"aga*
***inst the end"* O hole of**
skin ! porno lit's in roo
ts of f ire the "ran
dom" axis ,tom b numb
er Nine ,smoking~ lip≈
stuck agai nst les neiges
the end of h air the b
irth large and wet s
cripted on the st airs' p
aper b ricks ,the
cell-phone's end ,your f
oot again st that Blank
Cloud circling in the
centerfold ,lens and s
tocking *fk yourself your***
***anus worm ends* ,a toy**
s tore rubbed *agains t*

—John M. Bennett, Found in Ivan Argüelles'
Ars Poetica

www.ingramcontent.com/pod-product-compliance
Lightning Source LLC
Chambersburg PA
CBHW080532170426
43195CB00016B/2534
9780989157827